Walks in Mysterious Lancashire

Graham Dugdale

Published by Sigma Leisure – an imprint of
Sigma Press, 1 South Oak Lane, Wilmslow, Cheshire SK9 6AR, England.

British Library Cataloguing in Publication Data
A CIP record for this book is available from the British Library.

ISBN: 1-85058-691-8

Typesetting and Design by: Sigma Press, Wilmslow, Cheshire.
Printed by: MFP Design and Print

Cover photograph: Heysham Head from Sandilands Promenade
(Jon Sparks)
Maps and photographs: Graham Dugdale

Disclaimer: the information in this book is given in good faith and is believed to be correct at the time of publication. No responsibility is accepted by either the author or publisher for errors or omissions, or for any loss or injury howsoever caused. Only you can judge your own fitness, competence and experience.

Walk Validation
The walks in this book have been tested by Geoff Saunders, to whom both the author and publisher are grateful for his detailed comments and suggestions.

Prologue

*'Then, like the last priest of a vanished nation
The Shadow drew the cowl about its head,
And with a web-like hand made salutation,
And went back to the Dead.'*

Longfellow *'Shadow to Shadow'*

Intrigue, thwarted romance, superstition and all manner of skulduggery have long held a fascination for those who venture out beyond the confines of their own living room. The county of Lancashire lays claim to such a wealth of stories that this book is only able to scratch the surface.

Even though we might scoff at the notion that malicious witches stirred up a potent brew of spells atop Pendle Hill, the beliefs held by the eminent magistrates of 17th-century Lancashire are well documented and cannot be disputed. Reaching out from the grave, the influence of these much maligned harridans is still in evidence to this day, as I discovered at Woodplumpton where a floral tribute was left at the final resting place of 'The Fylde Witch', Meg Shelton.

Not all of the mysteries will despatch a chilled shiver of fear rippling down the spine, nor should you break out in a cold sweat at the thought of murder most foul having been committed in your own neighbourhood. Some are mere curiosities that have lain dormant until now, largely unknown even to locals.

The proverb declaring that 'you can't see the wood for the trees' is appropriate for those of us who take our own locality too much for granted. Pause awhile in Cowan Bridge, where Charlotte Brontë was inspired to create her epic novel about Jane Eyre; visit the holy waters of Fernyhalgh, whose recuperative powers have been garnered from divine inspiration; and commiserate with the fate of the legendary Cotton Tree at Sunderland Point before paying a wistful sojourn to the lonely grave of Sambo the Slave.

Perhaps these rambles will encourage more people to explore the county's hidden gems, all of them being within the capabilities of, dare I say it, the average walker. Only a handful entail any serious attempt at upward perambulation, ghosts and the like invariably being confined to the more populated lowlands. Such wraiths are sociable entities that prefer an audience when they deign to make an appearance.

From judges and dukes to toddlers and traffic wardens, the open countryside with its latent aura of mystery beckons invitingly for all to savour and enjoy. Don't be thwarted by inexplicable noises filtering down from the empty bedrooms of Melling Hall. Thumb your nose at the witches residing in Newchurch-in-Pendle. And by all means laugh at the Devil's stupidity in Cockerham. But, most of all, relish the high quality of walks on offer amidst the inimitable scenery of a county more usually remembered for its 'dark Satanic mills'. As you will discover, nothing could be further from the truth.

About the Walks

Graded according to geographical location, the walks fall into three general areas: North, Central and South Lancashire. As none of the high land visited exceeds the magical 2000-foot contour that would automatically confer mountain status, these are more akin to rambles than fell walks.

On very few of the routes did I meet other walkers, even though all followed rights of way established over centuries. This is how I prefer it but the consequence is that many of the paths are indistinct underfoot. Stiles are in the main well maintained, even where few travellers pass. For those who enjoy their own company and like to seek out new and exciting haunts, look no further. This is the book for you.

Although the Ordnance Survey has abandoned all pretence of retaining those measurements upon which the Empire was built, I steadfastly refuse to think metric. No enchanting association can be attached to a height of 557 metres. This seems a miserly altitude for the highest fell top visited, namely Pendle Hill. Far better, I think, to have climbed to a staggering 1827ft. This stubborn streak has been curtailed, however, in the written descriptions. More to encourage the modern walker to whom feet are those strange-shaped appendages that fit into your boots.

Another 'modern' feature that is appearing far too frequently these days in lowland pastures is the proliferation of the electric fence. This shocking piece of farm equipment is fast becoming a pain in the proverbial, both literally and otherwise. Those guardians of the land who provide stiles over their newly erected barriers are to be highly commended, but far too many are strung across existing rights of way. So beware!

Finally, a note about maps. Although my own hand-drawn sketch maps are sufficient to complete the walks, they could never entirely replace the relevant OS maps, which fill in the detail and provide a wider impression of the area being visited. OS 1:25 000 Pathfinder maps are currently being phased out in favour of the larger format Explorer series. Explorer maps for Lancashire are scheduled for the years 2000/2001.

Acknowledgements

Many thanks to Stephen Flowers of NeeBee Boots; Phil Ham of Lowe Aline in Kendal; Tom and Sandra Smith of First Terrace at Sunderland Point for providing shelter and sustenance when I was cut off by the tide. Also from Sigma Leisure, and highly recommended, is Kenneth Field's *Lancashire Magic and Mystery*. It looks in great detail at a whole host of strange and ghostly happenings within the county and makes an absorbing and thoroughly entertaining read.

Contents

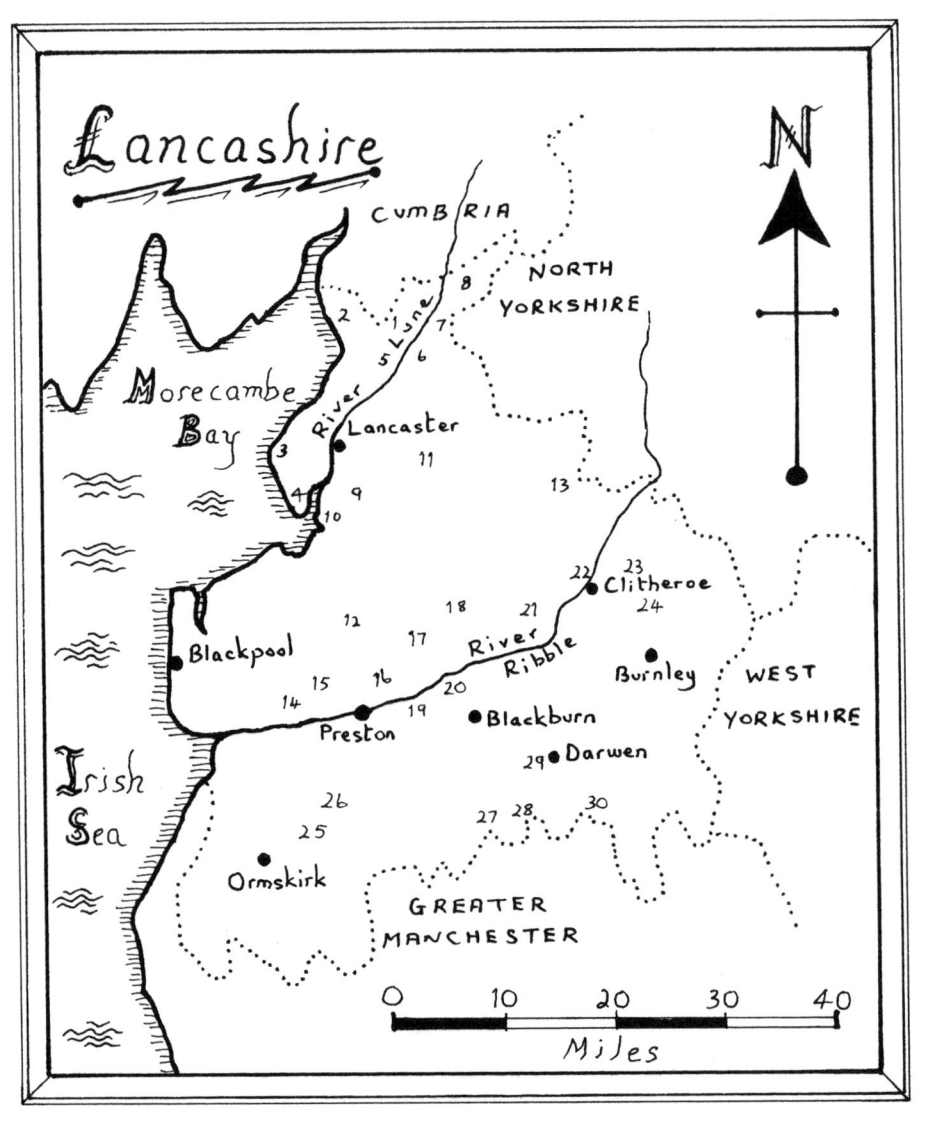

Locations of the walks

Key to Maps

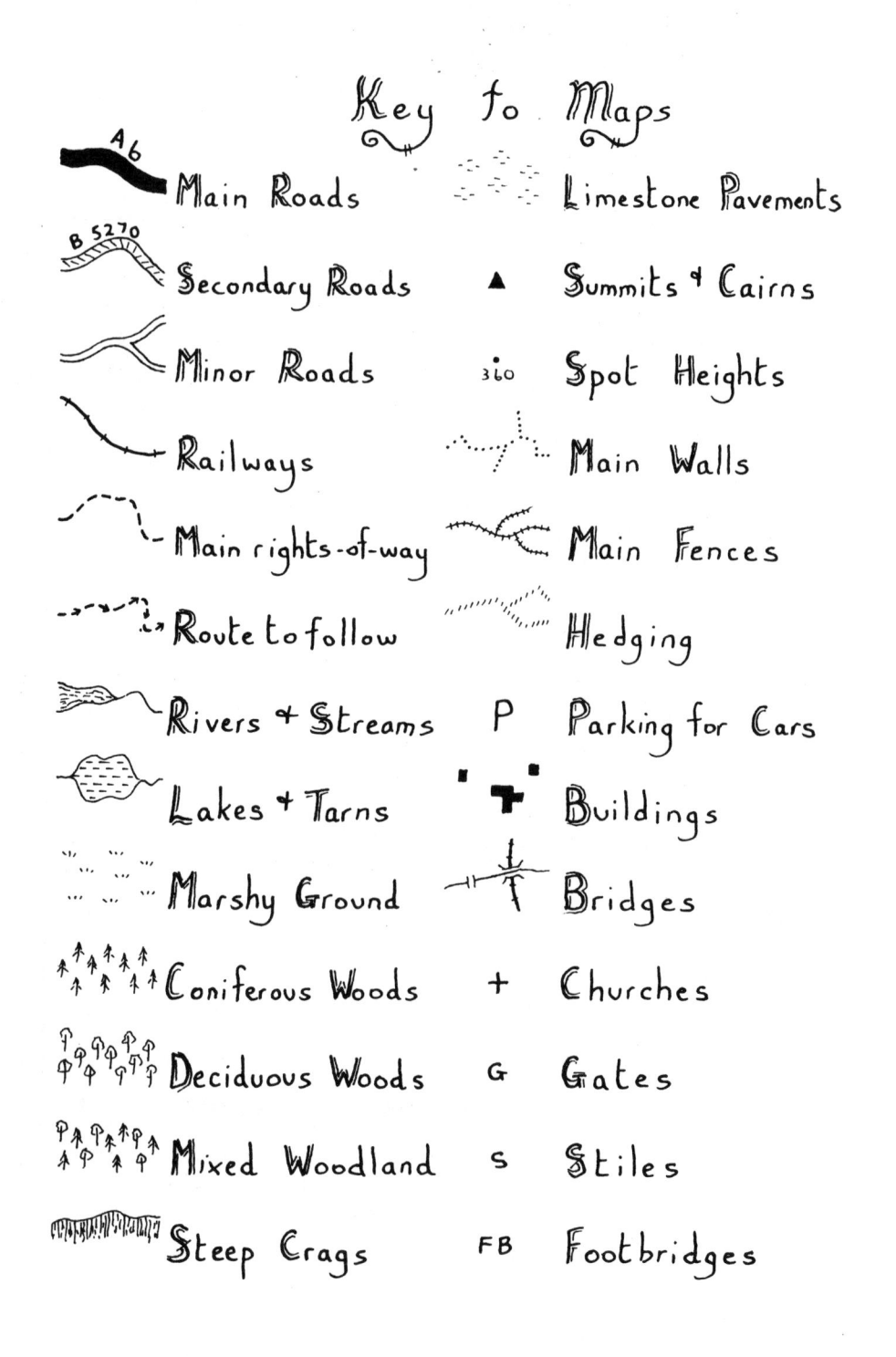

A6 Main Roads	Limestone Pavements
B 5270 Secondary Roads	▲ Summits & Cairns
Minor Roads	·360 Spot Heights
Railways	Main Walls
Main rights-of-way	Main Fences
Route to follow	Hedging
Rivers & Streams	P Parking for Cars
Lakes & Tarns	Buildings
Marshy Ground	Bridges
Coniferous Woods	+ Churches
Deciduous Woods	G Gates
Mixed Woodland	S Stiles
Steep Crags	FB Footbridges

Walk 1. Borwick

Wherein Walks the White Lady

Mystery: Borwick Hall GR 525730

Distance: 8½ miles

Total Height Climbed: 400 feet (122 metres)

Nearest Shops: Burton-in-Kendal

Start and Finish: Park on the rough track adjacent to where Borwick Hall Bridge crosses the Lancaster Canal immediately west of the village. Borwick itself has limited roadside parking close to the hall entrance.

Maps: Ordnance Survey 1:25 000 Pathfinder 637, Burton-in-Kendal and Caton; OS Outdoor Leisure 7, The English Lakes - South Eastern area.

Even during a busy bank holiday, when the Lake District is likely to be clogged with trippers, those who choose the undulating foothills of North Lancashire are guaranteed the seclusion denied the more popular honey pots. On the day I passed this way, no similar-minded ramblers were encountered – a recommendation in itself.

Clustered around the village green, stone cottages once occupied by a myriad of local tradesmen now provide high-profile residences for off-comers who commute to local towns. Yet there is no denying that Borwick exudes those characteristics one would expect from a classic English village. What sets it apart from others of similar mould is the hall whose battlemented walls dominate the surroundings.

Once a noble country seat of repute, Borwick Hall now acts as a residential outdoor pursuits centre under the control of Lancashire County Council. Although the central pele tower dates from the 14th century when such dour blockhouses were necessary for protection against marauding bands of insurgents, the main period of Borwick Hall's glory began in 1590. It was Robert Bindloss who expanded the gracious residence that he accrued with profits derived in the trading of Kendal cloth. As a royalist sympathiser, the third Sir Robert provided a haven for the future King Charles II after the crown fell to Cromwell's parliamentary army. Here it was that in 1651 the young prince dreamed of winning back his father's crown prior to fleeing into exile on the continent. During his brief sojourn at Borwick, Charles tarried awhile with a local girl, which led to the inevitable conclusion. He left soon after. But following his restoration to the throne, Charles remembered the product of his dalliance and made full provision for the child's future.

Most sinister of the Bindloss retainers was the family chaplain who refused to cut his beard after Charles I was executed in 1649. Richard Sherlock exercised an unhealthy influence over Sir Robert who was induced to persecute the 'New Puritanism' by breaking up meetings and abusing the participants.

Although the Lord of the Manor was said to be 'rich as any man in the north', he fell in with malign company which proved to be his undoing. No doubt his continued support of the royalist cause did nothing to improve his fortunes and, thereafter, Borwick Hall fell on hard times.

With regard to the mysterious element that has long emanated from the grey walls, we must return to its inception and the rascally Thomas Whittington. This callous rogue attempted to force his daughter into marrying a 'suitable husband' of his choosing. Her persistent refusal incensed Whittington, who imprisoned his wayward daughter in the high tower. And here it was that she remained, opting for a slow death from starvation rather than succumbing to her father's heinous demands. Known as 'The White Lady', the poor girl's ghost wanders the corridors of the pele tower searching for a means of escape from her incarceration. Even though most visitors have no knowledge of the legend, frequent sightings of the mystical figure clothed in white and sporting a wistful expression have been reported.

The Walk

On a busy bank holiday when I last visited the hall, it would appear that even The White Lady had elected to take a vacation as not a soul was in residence. So I headed east out of the village, taking the first signposted footpath on the left, which led over a grassy hillock down to St Mary's Church. Take a right from here past the memorial hall and along the lane to Priest Hutton.

Bear left then right at the village green to walk up a narrow lane until a rough track on the left is reached. About 100 metres along, mount a stile in the hedge on your right and slant up the rising slope to pass through a small wood. There is a stile at each end.

Thereafter, stick with the hedge on the right, ignoring an obvious

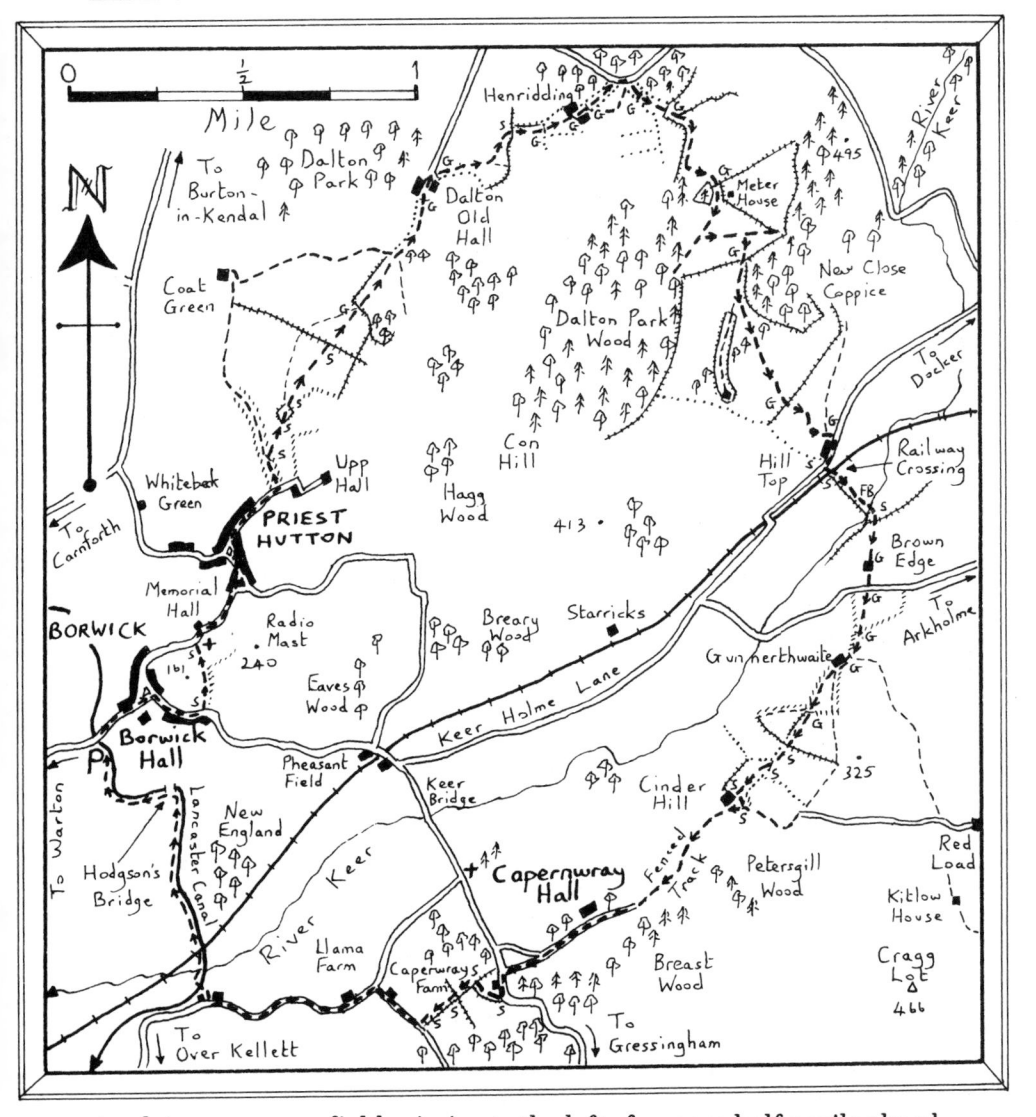

track to cross open fields aiming to the left of a copse half a mile ahead. An intervening fence stile will then bring you to a gate adjoining the wood. Continue ahead to merge with a major track from Coat Green and so on to Dalton Old Hall.

Pass through the farmyard and take a gate at the far side on the right, initially accompanying a wall along a churned-up track. Fork left off this to a concealed stile and then along a fence. Now overgrown, the original course of the path is clearly evident. Beyond a wall gate at the field corner, make a diagonal crossing to reach the dispersed farming settlement of Henridding. It is gated at either end of the yard.

Stick with the walled access track to the Burton-in-Kendal road. Bear right for 50 metres then fork right along another rough track. Follow this over rising ground between extensive stands of conifer plantings. Beyond the third gate, which follows an abrupt left-hander, take a right to another gate. Following this, the view opens out across the Keer Valley.

Ignore an oddly situated fenced corridor that appears ahead. Instead, keep left to trace an intermittent groove down the fellside, over a low knoll and so to a fence below. Beyond the gate, the path meanders down to Hill Top, passing through a gate at the left of the farm to emerge on Keer Holme Lane. Head right past the farm buildings to locate a hidden access point for crossing the railway track. Stop! Look! Listen! Providing a train driver with the opportunity to practise an emergency stop is not to be recommended.

Continue over the next field and a footbridge spanning the infant River Keer. Slant right over a fence stile and so across to Brown Edge. A gate allows passage through the farmyard to continue south. Cross a back lane through a gate and go along a path to the far side of the field. After the next gate, stroll along a hedge. At the end of the hedge a sharp right will bring you into the farmyard at Gunnerthwaite.

It is appropriate that this particular right of way connects a series of individual settlements along our side of the valley above the flood level. Care is needed after Gunnerthwaite at the end of the track that circles right. Our way forks left through a gate notable for the initials and dates of birth assigned to the makers, etched into the concrete posts.

Keep the fence on your right, mounting a stile ahead as you climb a gentle rise. Watch for an offset wall stile where the path continues on the far side of the wall to Cinder Hill. Slant left to cross this wall gap, then make an abrupt left turn to gain the rough lane via a gate. This amended route avoids the farmyard entirely.

Head along the fenced access track past the entrance to Cinder Hill. This becomes metalled on reaching Home Farm. Capernwray Hall appears on the right through trees soon after. Built in the early 19th century by George Marton, the High Sheriff of Lancaster, the hall is a magnificent example of baronial architecture at its most extravagant. Lavish attention has been paid to ensuring that the Martons enjoyed the highest level of luxury that their position demanded.

Borwick Hall and the surrounding estate were acquired in 1858. This was the family's period of greatest prosperity. Later its influence in society and fortunes declined. No Marton has lived at Capernwray since the Second World War and the hall was eventually auctioned in 1949. It was acquired by a Mr Thomas. His ambition to create an international bible school was certainly realised and today it is still a thriving community attracting young Christian students from all over the world.

On reaching the road from Borwick, take a left for 100 metres before joining a short enclosed passage on the right. There is a stile at either end. Bear left along a high fence and go over another stile before arriving at an even taller ladder stile. Cross a rough track behind Caperwray Farm and continue on to the lane serving a caravan park.

Lean right to merge with the Capernwray road then left past a breeding pad for llamas. These shy, retiring creatures are used for wool and as pack animals in their native South America. Keep a look out for them in the fields on the right.

Another half mile will bring you to Capernwray Old Hall where you should swing right to cross the Lancaster Canal bridge. Join the towpath heading north to cross a short aqueduct built by John Rennie in 1797 over the River Keer. A gentle stroll along this tranquil reach will soon return you to Borwick – and the culmination of a walk encompassing a pair of stately homes that will see out the century in a completely different guise from that in which they started it.

Capernwray Hall: now an international Bible school

Walk 2. Warton

Stars and Bars

Mysteries: The Washington Connection GR 498723;
Warton Crag Fort GR 492728

Distance: 4 miles

Total Height Climbed: 700 feet (213 metres)

Nearest Shops: Warton

Start and Finish: Park in the official car park located in an old
quarry 100 metres up the fell road, on the right of the George
Washington pub.

Map: Ordnance Survey 1:25 000 Pathfinder 636,
Grange-over-Sands

Should you elect to visit Warton near Carnforth in July, it may come as
something of a surprise to witness the flag of the United States waving
at you from the tower of St Oswald's church. July has always been a key
month for celebration in this remote village in North Lancashire. The
Stars and Stripes is raised above the village each Independence Day on
account of the American connection. For it was here that a close relative
of the first American president lived prior to 1750 and his departure for
a new life in Virginia. John Washington lived on Main Street in the
house that still bears his family name.

Transatlantic visitors are a common sight in July, Washington
House being an obvious focal point. A stroll down to the 15th-century
church passes the local pub. Always known as the Black Bull, it has recently undergone extensive refurbishment and been renamed the
George Washington.

The robust, square tower of St Oswald's was constructed in 1483 by
Robert Washington who chose a coat of arms described in heraldic lan-
guage as 'on a field argent, three mollets azure in chief, two bars gules.'
Originally part of the Washington memorial in the graveyard, centuries
of weathering have forced this sole remaining emblem of the family into
the tower, where it now resides permanently to prevent further erosion.

Washington House – home to the ancestor of the first president of the USA

Three mollets have since grown into fifty stars representing the number of states in the Union, the two bars have increased to thirteen which were the original member colonies that broke from the mother country to form the United States of America in 1776. And to think it all began in this small Lancashire village.

Another association through marriage can be traced which links the Washington family with the Churchills. It would appear, therefore, that the two great leaders were related. Anybody who can work out the exact relationship between Winston and George can have the honour of taking their esteemed guide out to lunch at the GW. Don't forget your credit card. Like our American cousins, I'm a big eater.

All the excitement generated by such a noble lineage should not detract from the Old Rectory opposite the church, which is Warton's most ancient building. Maintained by English Heritage, it was built by the Thweng Family and dates from the 14th century when warring factions sweeping down from the north dictated that such buildings should be heavily fortified.

Although now a shadow of its former glory, the Rectory offers a unique insight into the architecture of the period. It was the seat of law hereabouts until dispensing of justice later moved down the hill to the

Shovel Inn. This popular local pub was an important coaching inn on what used to be the main North-South route before it passed through Carnforth.

Straddling the lower slopes of a huge upthrust of limestone from which the village has acquired its name, Warton offers a ramble of superlative quality. Our route to the summit possesses all the attributes of a major fell walk in miniature – ideal for those who yearn to conquer Everest but cannot quite raise the necessary head of steam.

When approached from the direction of Kendal to the north, the fell is naught but a tree-girt ridge. Prosaic and barely worth a second glance, it makes no extrovert pretensions from this angle but places all of its goodies in the front window. From Morecambe Promenade the true grandeur of The Crag captures the eye magnificently and offers a shapely profile to the bay. It has the unmistakable appearance of a home-made gateau complete with layers of creamy filling. The insatiable appetite of industry, however, has resulted in a mammoth-sized bite of tasty limestone being snaffled from the southern flank. Thankfully, these activities have moved on to pastures new. But the scars still remain.

The Walk

From the car park now used as a training crag for rock climbers, ascend the stony track meandering through the dense tree cover to a sprung gate. Bear right then left along a limestone shelf that rises gradually across open ground to a stile above the vertical quarry face. Views to the west and south improve radically as height is gained.

An essential fence runs the length of the upper rim of the quarry, preventing an untimely demise of pets and papooses. A further 20 metres beyond the stile, lean right through open woodland to mount a series of layered terraces characteristic of the limestone terrain. After crossing an oddly placed stile, an acclivitous rock barrier is breached by an easy shelf rising to the upper tier. More adventurous hikers will find a suitably exacting route worthy of their undoubted prowess. Once above, it is but a simple task to gain the craggy citadel.

Exposed turrets of fluted grey guard the inner portal of what was a Brigantean stronghold in days of yore. Although it now sports a sylvan hat, there is no denying the impregnable nature of such a site. The southerly prospect across the broad expanse of salt marsh and sandy

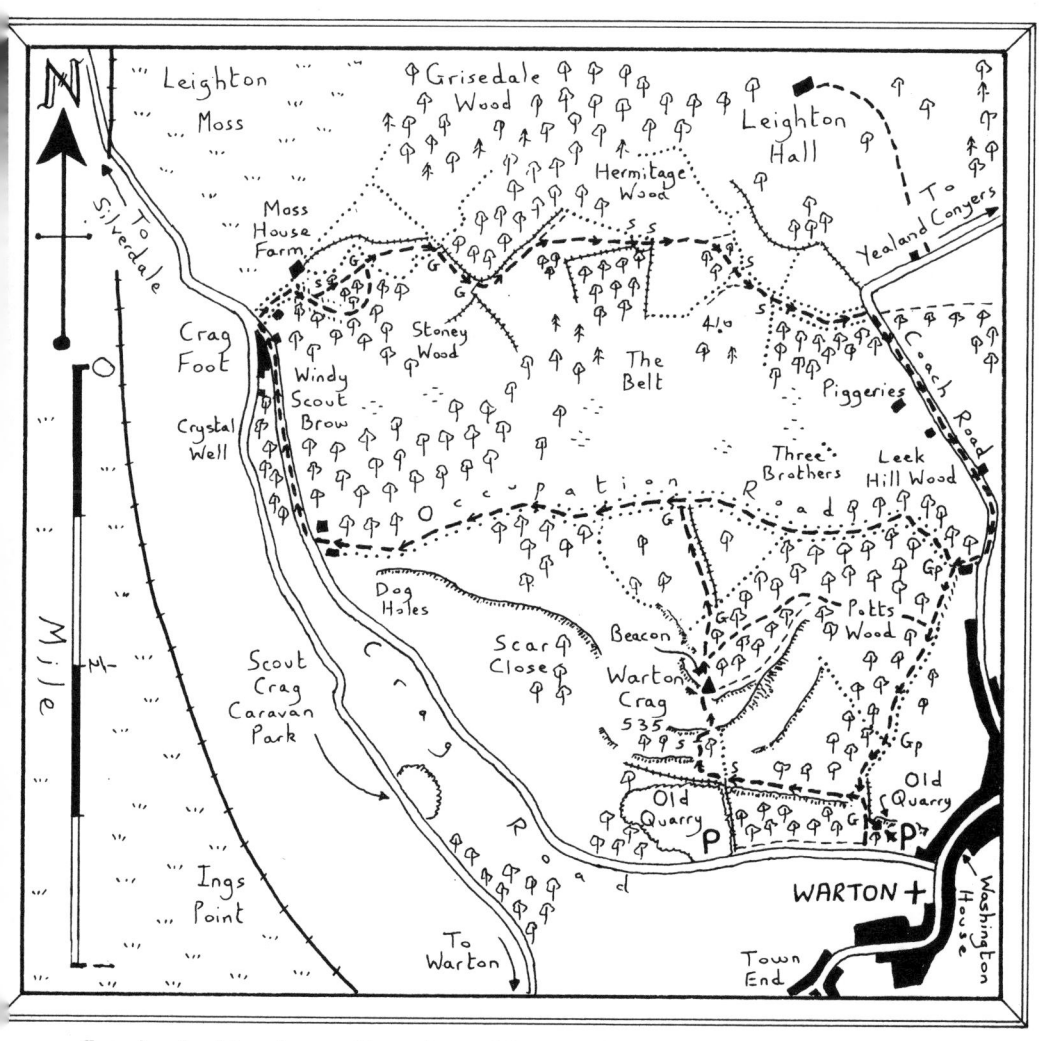

flats backed by the scalloped moulding of the Lakeland panorama is a joy to behold on a summer's evening.

Concealed within the clutch of trees occupying the summit domain is a concrete trig column. But it is a steel basket mounted on a wooden plinth that commands our attention. This beacon was erected and lit in 1988 to mark the 400th anniversary of the Spanish Armada being sighted. This was the 16th-century method of alerting the country to the danger of an invasion that thankfully failed to materialise.

As a short climb of considerable merit Warton Crag is unequalled, its

modest height in no way detracting from the sense of isolation and re-
moteness normally associated with much loftier peaks. The claim that
you cannot make a mountain out of a molehill is most assuredly challenged in this instance. For many, it will be their only fell conquest, and
who can deny them the laudable status of such an achievement.

Turn your back on the dramatic panorama to head north into the tree
cover, taking a left fork at the signpost. Pass down a gentle slope and
through a gate into open country where a fence is accompanied down to
Occupation Road. This walled track crosses the fell from east to west.
Head left down to Crag Road and then right down to Crag Foot, where
the road skirting the lower reaches of Warton Crag is joined. Take the
access track serving Moss House Farm then slant right up another after
100 metres. Watch for a stile on the left giving entry to a wood.

A thin path brings you to a gate at the far side where a clear track
crosses the irregular-shaped field. Our way curves right through a gate
and along an enclosed corridor. At its top end, bend left along a fence to
a gate. Keep the fence on your left until a small copse is reached. Fork
half right to cross to the far right corner of the field. Here a pair of fence
stiles 50 metres apart will bring you to a field of open woodland. Continue ahead for 100 metres until a path swings right beneath the verdant
canopy to mount a grass slope to a wall gap clearly in view ahead.

Merge with a major field track to follow the wall on your left and pass
over a stile into a walled passage. Walk down this then turn right down
Coach Road. After half a mile, make another right up Occupation Road.
Proceed for no more than 50 metres until passage through a wall gap
can be made on the left.

Accompany the clear path as it soon slants in to join a wall around
the lower edge of Warton Crag. Winding in charming fashion through
the dense cloak of coppice woodland, this part of the crag lies within a
nature reserve which aims to protect the flora and fauna that is unique
to this locale. Watch for the sprung gate on your left for the return to the
car park.

For those of us who live within site of Warton Crag, it will always be
a firm favourite. Perhaps our American visitors will come to appreciate
that the best in life does not necessarily have to be the biggest.

Walk 3. Heysham

Hauntings

Mysteries: The County Library GR 417617;
St Patrick's Chapel GR 408618; Heysham Moss

Distance: 4½ miles

Total Height Climbed: Insignificant

Nearest Shops: Heysham

Start and Finish: Ample parking space is available on the official site adjacent to Half Moon Bay and is free of charge.

Map: Ordnance Survey 1:25 000 Pathfinder 648, Morecambe

Although not regarded as an integral part of this walk, the County Library at Higher Heysham, near to the Strawberry Gardens, lies on the route to Half Moon Bay. Pause for a while outside this Edwardian building to reflect on the unexplained vibes to be found within. Mysteries of a distinctly uncanny nature are more likely to elicit a cold shiver than those lined up along the shelves.

Enter if you must. After all, it's only a library, isn't it? So what harm can it do? But strange happenings fit to make the knees tremble and the blood run cold have been reported on more than one occasion. Mournful cries of anguish, such as those from some poor soul in torment; sudden appearances of spectral apparitions; and even the books moving of their own volition as if under the direction of a resident poltergeist have all been experienced.

My own mother has on more than one occasion 'felt a presence' in the reading room: a sudden drop in temperature on a hot summer's day and, just for the briefest instant, the mood of someone or something passing through on a higher plane. Invisible but there nonetheless. Could this have been due to a ghost? Surely the unlimited supplies and avid consumption of romantic fiction cannot be blamed.

On one occasion, the librarian was about to close when she noticed a man sitting in the reading room. On returning to inform him of the imminent closure, he had vanished. With no other exits from the room, what had happened to him? A trick of the light, or something a little more obscure? Who can tell?

Talk of a little old man with grey hair and dressed in tweeds acting like a Will o' the Wisp might well have its origins behind the bar of the Strawberry Gardens Inn down the road. Please ensure that any of these kinds of spirits are reserved for the end of the walk, assuming of course that the Heysham Moss Boggarts let you pass unmolested.

These and other happenings have assured the Haunted Library of an unsavoury reputation that shows no inclination to disappear. As to the origin of these ghostly events, a dark and vehement past appears to point the right direction. The suggestion that a guilty conscience regarding an overdue book is to blame must have been delivered with tongue firmly embedded in cheek.

The Walk

If you succeed in evading the sticky fingers of the phantom of the day, continue onward to Half Moon Bay for the start of the walk. From the car park, take a stroll along the short promenade before dropping down onto the shingle beach. After rounding the rocky promontory ahead, a chaotic splay of sea-washed boulders makes for a stimulating if somewhat precarious route along the shoreline. Avoid the rocks coated in seaweed, which will upend you in no uncertain fashion. Small caves have been excavated from the brittle cliffs whose crumbly nature is evident from the rock-strewn beach.

A fine example of an anticline can be seen along the steep cliff face below Heysham Head. Geologists always look out for these arched features in the Earth's strata when searching for new oil fields. Deposits are most commonly found secreted below such domed formations. Unlike those in the Gulf region of the Middle East, however, the Heysham anticline is a mere tiddler.

Beyond is a complex of gnarled bulwarks thrusting out into the bay. When vertical cliffs extended all the way round the headland, there was a magnificent cave under the grassy sward here. It was a magnetic attraction for we youngsters, but clearly dangerous. Perhaps it was fortuitous that nobody was inside when the inevitable collapse occurred.

Today there is no steeply canting rock face to negotiate as you climb up onto Barrow's Field. Ahead, perched on the rocky point stands, St Patrick's Chapel, or what remains of it. Surely, no other religious edifice commands such an imposing situation. Legend suggests it was erected

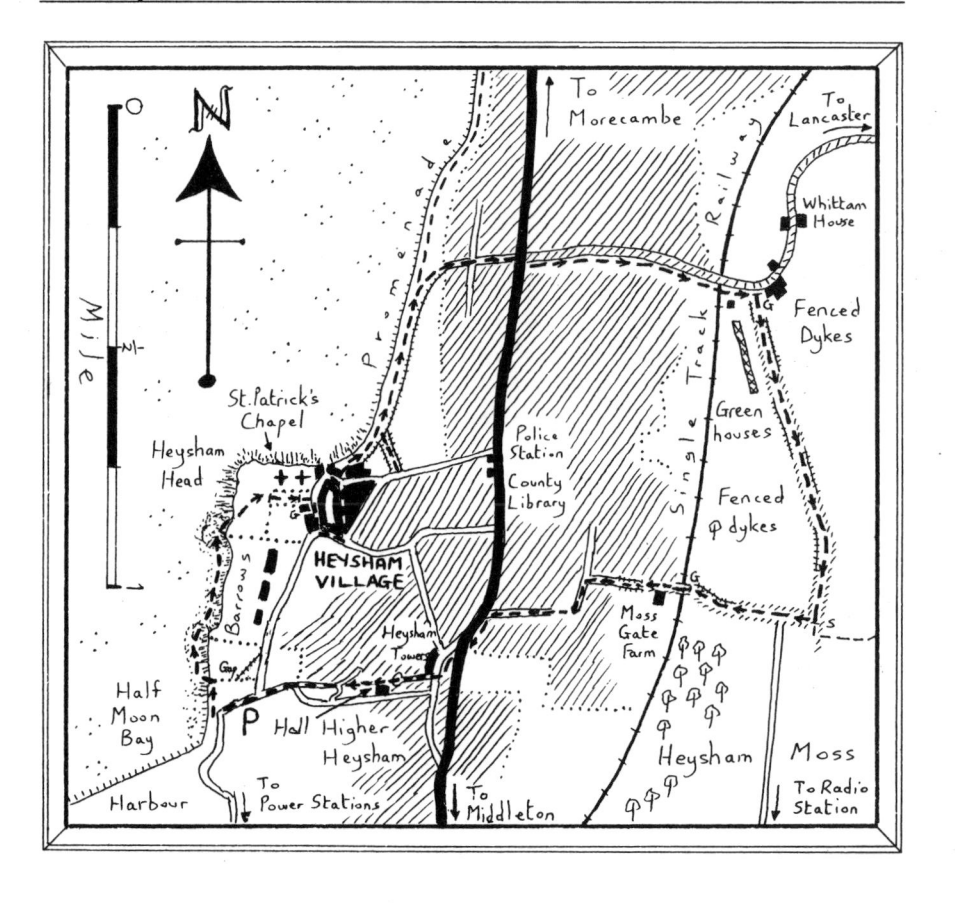

on the site where the Irish saint first landed, along with that country's only poisonous snake. Such a lonely outpost must indeed have been ideal for the faithful to pursue a life of piety and prayer. Yet when the rampant seas hammered at the rugged headland and set their teeth on edge, doubtless an extra plea for deliverance was despatched upstairs.

Dated at around AD800, the six narrow coffins hewn from the solid rock have made the site unique in archaeological circles. Only higher order residents will have been granted the privilege of interment, lesser mortals being consigned to Barrow's Field. It is regarded as the finest Neolithic site in Northern Europe. Remains unearthed in the vicinity of the chapel have been reburied in the churchyard below.

Resume the walk by passing through a gap in the wall crossing

Heysham Head, so dropping down to visit St Peter's Church. Enjoying a
Saxon heritage, this ancient, stone house of God is no less impressive.
Few similar establishments are able to capture the mood of antiquity
that permeates the ozone hereabouts.

The Millennium anniversary of the church's founding took place in
1967 and embroidered hassocks provide a contemporary reflection of a
long and diverse pedigree. Perhaps the most intriguing element relates
to the Viking era, when Torrig, who gave his name to the Morecambe
suburb of Torrisholme, settled here.

Legend suggests that the hog's back stone (now inside the church to
preserve it from climatic assault) was a memorial from the Norse chief-
tain to a respected Saxon adversary called Eagle. Although others can
be seen at Penrith and Gosforth in Cumbria, no other is so well preserved. Intricate carvings make for a fascinating insight into the eternal
conflict between the forces of light and dark, the good and evil sides of
life as perceived in the 10th century.

Whilst ambling around these primeval relics, you would do well to
heed the salient advice offered by the Friends of Heysham Barrows:

* Do not leave anything but footprints

* Do not kill anything but time

* Do not take anything but photographs

Now absorbed into the greater mass that is Morecambe, the old village
of Heysham still retains a distinctly proud identity. It is clear where the
newer encroachment begins once you have turned right to walk up
Main Street. Fishing was the prime source of employment for centuries
until tourism eventually took over. Main Street extends right down to
the sea, enabling the fishermen to trundle their handcarts onto the sand
flats and out to the shellfish beds a mile out into the bay.

Once in the open square, swing left at the post office to walk down
Bailey Lane. This is the epitome of old world charm and is complete
with the fishermen's cottages, one of which was my first home after I
was married. Prior to rejoining Main Street at the bottom, bear right up a
narrow ginnel on to the cliff path.

Enjoy the promenade walk for half a mile before leaning right to join
Whinnysty Lane. This is New Heysham, heavily built up with undistin-
guished mid-century villas arranged in geometric rows. Hurry through
this urban sprawl, crossing straight over Heysham Road at the traffic
lights and continuing along the right pavement of Oxcliffe Road for a
further half mile.

Stone coffins at Heysham Head, overlooking Barrows Field

The final 200 metres of this section, where the single track railway is bridged, requires care as no footways are provided. Immediately over the bridge, take the first right along Clay Lane. This is initially metalled and a welcome relief as it forges straight into the heartland of Heysham Moss.

At one time a turgid morass of clinging marsh and oozing mud, pockets of settlement were restricted to the isolated 'clay islands' that always poked above the flood plain. Inherent danger from rising water spawned numerous tales concerning the presence of fearful denizens that roamed the marsh seeking out lost travellers.

Spectres, goblins and stroppy boggarts haunted the swampy morass, playing havoc with the nerves of those forced to traverse this unsavoury reach. One is said to be the ghost of a local lad called Billy Brown who became ensnared by the grasping tendrils of marsh grass and was finally sucked under. Much of Higher Heysham has disappeared under a creeping expanse of concrete that has tended to drive the apparitions away in search of a more lucrative environment elsewhere.

What remains of the Moss today has been effectively drained by a dense network of dykes that help keep it relatively dry. Ideal for the grazing of sheep and cattle, it is still too wet for the cultivation of crops.

Clay Lane bears sharp right to cross over the single-track railway through a gate. Pass the sad remains of Moss Gate Farm on the left, much of whose land has been given over to modern housing. Climb above the Moss where the rough track now merges into Abingdon Grove. At its end, continue ahead along a fenced track between houses to a T-junction.

Bear left following the right of way signs and then right soon after along another unmade path. Join Heysham Mossgate Road. At its end, head left along Heysham Road and almost immediately right past the Old Hall Inn. Follow Old Road left past the stone-fronted dwellings of Heysham Towers, which still exude a sense of nostalgia from its colourful past as a holiday camp, a reminder of the resort's vibrant heyday.

Turn right up Heysham Hall Grove, a short cul-de-sac that tapers into a narrow paved footway passing to the right of Heysham Hall. Built in 1839 as a manor house, it was transformed into a hotel in 1922, and has now been converted into private apartments. The suggestion that a medieval dungeon complete with connecting tunnel is concealed somewhere in the grounds has never been verified.

Continue past the hall and go right and left down Cyprus Road to where it merges with Smithy Lane. Keep ahead back to Half Moon Bay, the view now dominated by the twin towers of the Heysham nuclear power stations.

Walk 4. Sunderland

Beware the Lunar Tides

Mysteries: The Cotton Tree GR 427558;
Sambo's Grave GR 422559

Distance: 4 miles

Total Height Climbed: Nil

Nearest Shops: Overton

Start and Finish: At the end of the road serving the village of
Sunderland across Lades Marsh. Pull onto the shingle in front of
the public conveniences.

Map: Ordnance Survey 1:25 000 Pathfinder 659, Galgate and
Dolphinholme

Warning: The road across Lades Marsh is subject to flooding by the
tides surging up the Lune Estuary. Ensure that you are aware of the appropriate times before setting out on this walk.

Surely there can be no other settlement that quite compares to
Sunderland. Not, I hasten to add, the home of the red and whites at
Roker Park. This tiny enclave lies on the leeward shore of a promontory
forming one of the jaws at the mouth of the River Lune.

Like a blunted dagger stabbing at the flat expanse of Cockerham
Sands, Sunderland remains a fragment of the distant past transplanted
into the 20th century. Tidal flooding that effectively cuts the village off
by road at regular intervals ensures an ethereal mysticism that has created a magnetic fascination for this particular visitor at least. The villagers positively encourage the sense of isolation that lifts Sunderland
above other possible comparisons. Although the ships that made the
name of Sunderland a byword in maritime circles no longer tie up at the
stone jetty, other time-honoured professions continue.

Fishing and agriculture still provide employment for numerous residents, the river being cleaner today than at any time in living memory.
Whitebait, sprats and flounder, together with the ubiquitous salmon,
find their way into nets strung across the estuary.

Before the Lune was made navigable, ships from the Americas unloaded cargoes of tobacco, sugar and, of course, cotton. These were then packed over the marshes to Lancaster. Indeed, Sunderland was the first port in the country to import raw cotton, an essential ingredient of the Industrial Revolution. But once ships were able to disgorge into the more sheltered harbour of Glasson Dock after 1787, Sunderland rapidly declined in importance.

The Walk

Making your way south along the unmade track fronting the quayside, the residential housing of First Terrace is soon passed. Continue past The Lane along the narrow causeway which connects with Second Terrace. Most of the buildings in this part of the village are of three storeys and were originally warehouses. This was the main dock, the initial building on the left being known as the Bath House. A delousing shed for 'lively' matelots, it later became a changing room for bathers in a more genteel period of the village's history.

At the end of the block are the remains of the legendary Cotton Tree. After 250 years of constant growth, it finally succumbed to the ravages of time by giving up the ghost on New Year's Day of 1998. Opinion differs as to its lineage. Some claim it is a kapok seed dropped by one of the sailors and left to sprout, others that it is a Black Poplar of European extraction. Its prestige was such that a ground lintel was placed over the roots for protection when the current dwelling was erected in the mid-18th century. Once a familiar landmark regarded with much affection, its waving fronds jogged by the steady beat from the prevailing westerlies provided locals with a stabilising reminder of their poignant heritage. Today, only a stump remains of this ancient relic.

Sunderland Point itself forms the southern tip of the blade and is fast being worn away by the strong tidal flow. Urgent action is needed to prevent further erosion if this unique environment is to be preserved in tact.

Return to The Lane, passing a line of upright stakes from which linen fishing nets were hung up to dry before they were replaced by nylon. Bear left along the walled track to its far end on the western side of the promontory. Salt marsh occupies the foreground, acting as a buffer against the constant threat of flooding. Head left for 150 metres until you reach a short flight of stone steps that give access to the fenced enclosure containing a small grave. This is where a West Indian slave named Sambo was buried after passing away on arrival at Sunderland.

A stone slab, often adorned with mementoes from local school children, marks his final resting-place. Some say he died of loneliness after being abandoned by his master. Others claim drunken revellers who frequented the two inns in the village murdered him.

In those days, death was a solitary affair for Negroes, who were not considered suitable for a Christian burial. Perhaps a fitting tribute from those who pass this way would be to ponder over the distressing circumstances that led to such an austere locale being chosen. Thankfully, we have come a long way since the days when human beings were treated as chattels to be bought and sold at will.

One thing is for certain. Sambo has become far more renowned in death than he ever was in life. Could that be considered sufficient recompense? I think not. A brass plaque affixed to the plain slab has a touching verse in dedication. It was written in 1796 and a sample is repeated here:

'Full sixty years the angry winter's wave
Has, thundering dashed this bleak and barren shore
Since Sambo's head laid in this lonely grave
Lies still and ne'er will hear their turmoil more.'

From this special place, head north along the edge of the shoreline. It is lined with gorse and the occasional wind-bent tree. The reinforced buttressing along Alderley Bank provides welcome flood control for the farmland behind.

Continue along the clear route to Potts Corner, where alders flourish and where the Lord of the Manor still has the right to collect right-of passage fees from vehicular traffic. It is one of only seven such holdings in the country. Cars have now replaced horse-drawn vehicles at the end of the road connecting with Middleton.

Walk up the meandering highway for half a mile until a signpost points the way eastwards towards Middleton. After 100 metres cross a stile, keeping the hedge on your right. Beyond the next stile, veer to the right to yet another. Here, cross the field, keeping left of Trumley Farm as you go over a fence stile and down to one breaking through the thick hedge. Take a right along the access road from Marsh Lea to a T-junction. Lean right along the parallel, metalled lanes with unusual stiles. Officially, you should cross to the far side and rejoin 150 metres ahead at the private entrance to Trailholme. The right of way then circles round to the right of the house, through a gate and aiming for the embankment in front.

New wooden fencing and ladder stiles must be negotiated to con-

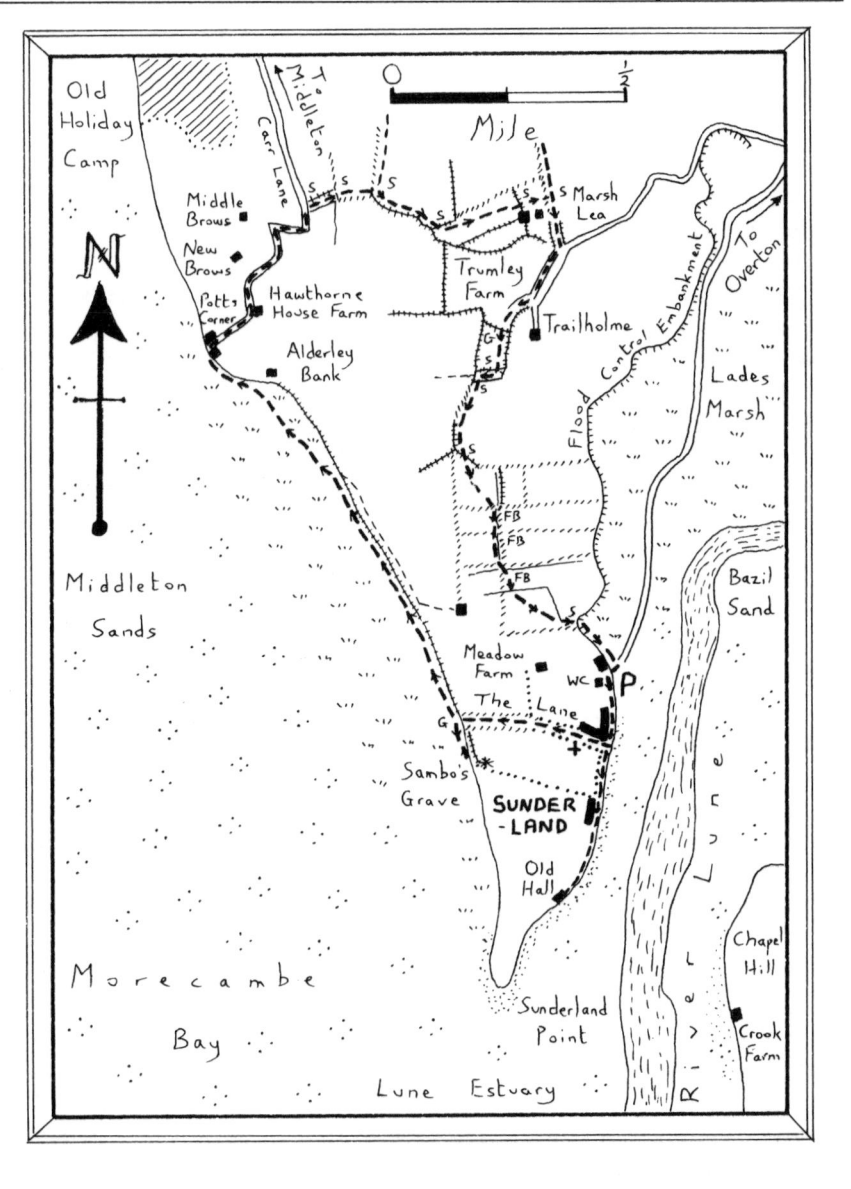

tinue. Mount the embankment, descend to the other side and so enter an adjoining field. Do **not** use the stiles which lead back to the embankment. Instead, proceed alongside the hedge and the continuing fence until a stile is reached. Stroll across the next field to the far-left corner,

The lonely grave of Sambo, who died at Sunderland Point

where a footbridge over a dyke is utilised. Keep a hedge on your left to cross two more footbridges, the last one spanning a junction of dykes. Stick with the watercourse, now on the right, before slanting half left to the far corner of the field.

A set of steps leads to the main tidal barrier, where a last fence stile is crossed. Walk back to the edge of Sunderland and take note of the wide range of craft moored hereabouts. Providing you have taken due heed of the tide tables published in local papers such as the Morecambe Visitor and Lancaster Guardian, driving back over Lades Marsh should pose no problems. Your sagacious guide was not so astute on his most recent visit and ended up being cut off for three hours as Sunderland became a virtual island, at least to road vehicles.

The Bell and Ship Inns have long been converted to residences, but a warm friendly community still remains. The sense of isolation appears to draw residents close together in mutual support against the elements; a consideration that is transferred to visitors who find themselves inadvertently stranded.

My sincere thanks to those who gave from the heart.

Walk 5. Aughton

Lunar Module

Mystery: The Aughton Pudding GR 550673

Distance: 7½ miles

Total Height Climbed: 450 feet (137 metres)

Nearest Shops: Caton

Start and Finish: Parking in the village of Aughton is limited. You are, however, unlikely to be caught in a traffic jam (unless of course it is Pudding Day).

Map: Ordnance Survey 1:25 000 Pathfinder 637,Burton-in-Kendal and Caton; OS Outdoor Leisure 41, Forest of Bowland & Ribblesdale.

Nobody who passes through it can deny that Aughton (pronounced Afton) lies in a time warp. Little has changed here in centuries. Indeed, the first new building in 200 years was erected in the 1930s and caused such a stir as to be worthy of inclusion in the local paper. Even today, only the odd bungalow has been added, blending harmoniously into a characteristic fusion of stone.

Traffic is non-existent, the only hold-ups likely to be from sheep crossing the narrow lane. A triangle of grass marks the core of this tiny enclave that boasts neither shop nor pub yet at one time boasted a prestigious grammar school. One could be forgiven for wondering how such a settlement came to exist here in the first place.

Farming was clearly the principal activity from the earliest times and still is. But one traditional craft developed which was to put Aughton on the map, effectively securing it a permanent place in history. Basket-making might not immediately conjure up visions of national acclaim, though here lies the source of the village's renown. Willow reeds grown along the banks of the Lune were first heated in a large cauldron to make them supple. On one occasion a local wag remarked that the circular container would make 'a gurt pudding boiler'.

This idle comment started a certain William Lamb thinking that just such an idea could benefit the village.

In consequence, he announced the preparation of a plum pudding to be cooked in a cauldron measuring six feet by two feet. The event duly took place in the year 1781 and was reconvened every twenty-one years thereafter. The most disastrous of the concoctions occurred in 1845. The finished product was so hard that it had to be rolled down the steep flank of Aughton Brow, there to be broken up with pick axes.

After 1886 the proceedings were discontinued until the splendid resurrection of 1971. The most recent preparation of the giant pudding was rather a damp squib due to the inclement weather, although the end product was well up to standard. Weighing in at a record 7190lbs and mixed in a concrete mixer with the registration PUD 1N, let us hope this tasty tradition will have an equally successful result in 2013.

The Walk

Our walk begins by heading north up the hill road for 100 metres. Enter a field on your left by a stile. Take a west-south-westerly bearing as you slant across the grassy brow, climbing three stiles on the approach to Far Highfield.

Casting a weather eye to the north-east up the Lune Valley, Ingleborough's table-top profile controls the skyline. Like a Carthaginian galley of old, it cleaves a passage through the rippling waves of limestone pavement. Closer to home, and far less impressive, the billowing plume of smoke from Claughton Manor Brick Works pumps forth from the aluminium chimney. Even on a Sunday, it would appear, the wheels of industry revolve unhindered.

Just beyond a footbridge, pass right of a square building in the middle of the field. Too small for human endeavour, one can only speculate as to its true use. Beyond the stile abutting the farm, maintain a course parallel with the fence before aiming for a field corner on the right. Keep the hedge on your right over two stiles to arrive at Middle Highfield.

At this farm, an amalgam of buildings needs to be circumvented using a total of eight barriers if progress is to be continued. Easy to follow, the order of negotiation is as follows: stile, stile, gap, gate, stile, stile, gate, stile. Counting them off successfully will bring you to a marker post at the far side.

Accompany a wall through a gate and then along a fence to the terminus of the field. Mount a stile to cross the next field corner and go through a gate. Lean right across to the far side and follow the hedge round to Lower Highfield, which is located on a spring line in a depression. Follow the upper rim of a banking to pass left of the farmhouse.

After passing through three gates, accompany a fence for 100 metres down to a gate at the higher limit of a wooded glen. Keep the next fence on your left before entering the wood via an iron kissing gate. Pass between the open ranks of coniferous trees to exit via a similar gate at the far side. Cross to a corner where the hedge is in the process of reconstruction between parallel fences.

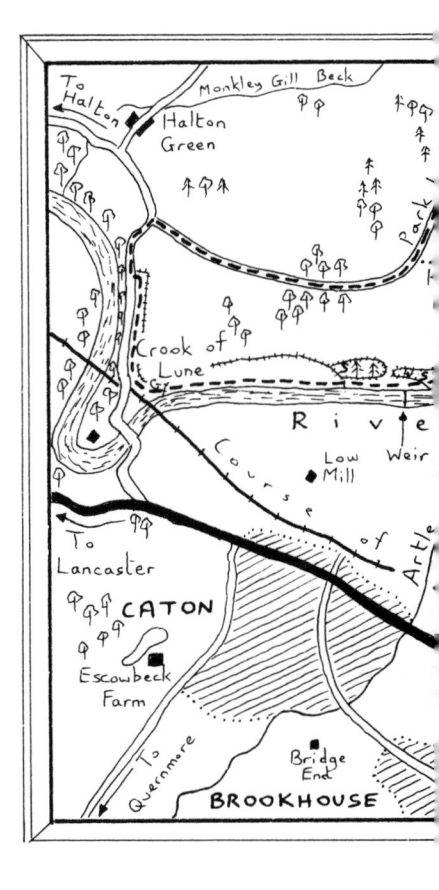

Keep to its left side until a short corridor is reached. There is a stile at either end. Below stands the austere mansion of Halton Park. Sombre and forbidding, its thick walls appear to pulsate with esoteric awareness. Certainly this dour-looking residence would make a splendid backdrop for ghostly appearances. Unfortunately, I have failed to unearth any such irregularities. Perhaps local readers will have more knowledge in this respect. I await your calling with avid relish.

Slant left down a grass banking to meet a track serving Hawkshead Farm. Bear right along this, down to the estate road. Turn left along the metalled lane. Walled initially, it soon opens out into wide, grass parkland sloping down to the banks of the Lune.

At the edge of the park, pass through a pair of stone gateposts and bear left. Keep to the left pavement, which soon gives access to a path on the far side of the road wall. The Crook of Lune is reached after a quarter of a mile. For over two centuries this beauty spot encompassing a hairpin loop in the River Lune has attracted visitors. Turner was inspired to paint the arched span, which was later to be paralleled by a railway bridge. The original Penny Bridge was replaced by the present structure

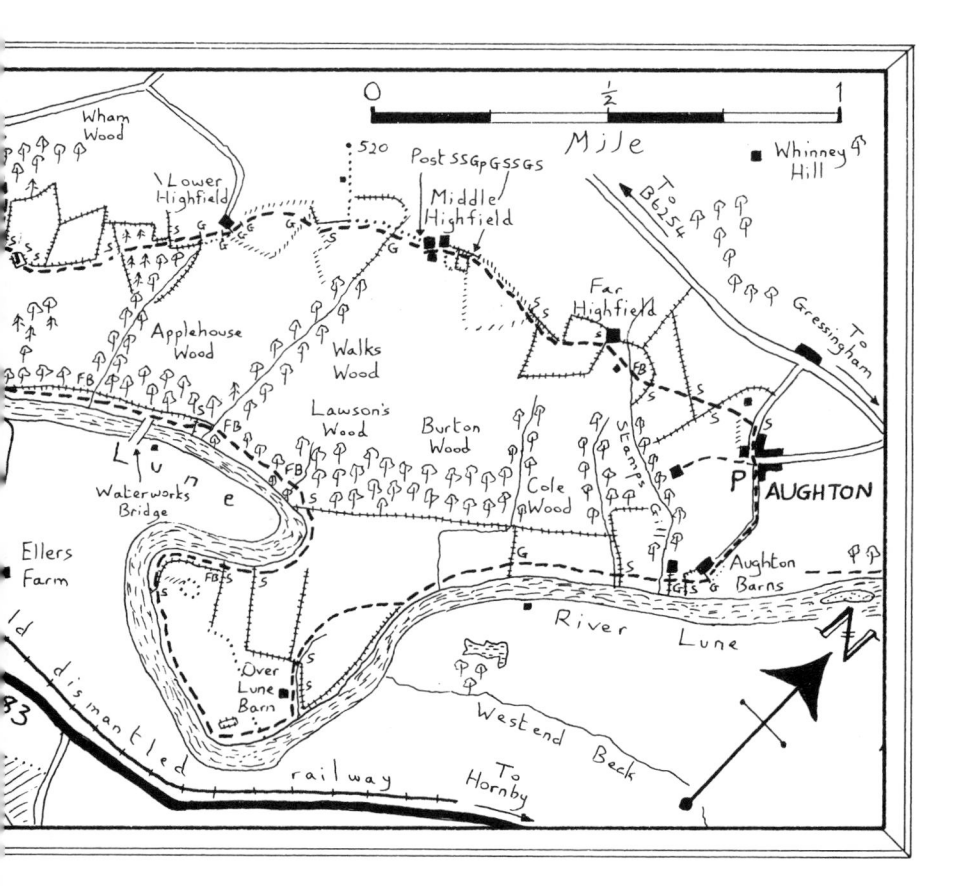

in 1883 after its central portion collapsed. It is still popular with locals, especially on a sunny afternoon when picnics are a favoured pastime along the verdant terracing.

Our way lies upriver along the broad left-hand terrace. Take note of Low Mill, the large, gaunt building on the far shore. Once a thriving cotton mill, it has now been converted into living accommodation. Thomas Hodgson built it in 1784. Half his labour force comprised young orphans brought in from the slums of Liverpool. Unlike many of his contemporaries, Hodgson treated his workers fairly. Although a strict employer, he kept the youngsters well clothed and fed.

Ranged along the skyline of Caton Moor, the growth of wind turbines is a reminder of the changing nature of our energy supply. Water wheels gave way to coal and steam power, which in turn has been superseded

Aughton, where a giant pudding is made every twenty-one years

by electricity generation. Yet even experimentation with renewable sources of energy such as wind causes controversy from those who claim such devices are a blot on the natural landscape.

After crossing two stiles the riverside path enters the woodland fringe that washes its roots in the gentle waters. Emerging into an open stretch, a footbridge is crossed. Soon after the waterworks' bridge is passed. Enter Applehouse Wood, where the path climbs above the river on this steep northern flank. At the far side, a flight of steps leads down to a stile at the edge of the wood.

This is where we follow the broad sweep of the river in a wide arc for 1½ miles, making only a quarter mile in actual progress. These loops are often to be found in the mature mid-sector of river valleys. Material is deposited on the inner bend where the water flow is slowest. It is the outer edge where erosion of the sides is most pronounced. Eventually, the river will cut through the neck, straightening itself and leaving an oxbow lake.

Walkers who suddenly remember their wedding anniversary and the need to visit a florist might well be tempted to cut across the intervening neck of land at the edge of Burton Wood. Naturally, I could not possibly comment on such activity nor condone it.

So push on round to the first fence stile, which is followed by another after 100 metres. The path is then directed into the Lune's sandy flood gullies. A little while later, cross back onto the raised platform by another stile and continue following the river. After passing a fenced enclosure, a broken wall is crossed. Aim for the right side of Over Lune Barn, so-named because those who made use of this solid building had to cross 'over the Lune' from the Caton side. Beyond the next fence stile, 100 metres ahead, make a wide parabola to the right and back towards the river's edge.

As the next gated barrier is neared, it is clear that efforts are afoot to prevent further inroads into the riverbank at this point. Make your way along the clear track to Aughton Barns where a steep climb out of the valley bottom is needed for the return to the village. On this most acclivitous section of the walk, one can but sympathise with the smallholder living in this isolated settlement during a severe winter when the road freezes over.

Walk 6. Hornby

Towers of Strength

Mysteries: Hornby Castle GR 588686;
Monteagle Tower GR 585686

Distance: 8½ miles

Total Height Climbed: 600 feet (183 metres)

Nearest Shops: Hornby

Start and Finish: Arriving from the direction of Lancaster, take note
that a free car park is provided on the left of the A683, where it
crosses the River Wenning in Hornby.

Maps: Ordnance Survey 1:25 000 Outdoor Leisure 41, Forest of
Bowland & Ribblesdale; OS Outdoor Leisure 2, Yorkshire Dales -
Southern & Western areas; short stretch on OS Pathfinder 638.

One correspondent made the witty observation that the designer of
Hornby Castle might well have possessed a touch of Disney magic in his
blood. And driving along the Lune Valley from the direction of Lancaster, one can certainly accede to such an opinion.

But a fairytale castle beloved of Disneyland, it is not. Defensively situated within a bend of the River Wenning and protected by steep cliffs,
it has been utilised by generations of settlers in search of a safe base
from which to operate. The Viking warrior Horni, who gave his name to
the village, was one of numerous warlords to appreciate the protective
nature of the site.

After repulsing the incursions of various invaders, the castle earned
a well-deserved reputation as an impregnable stronghold. Ensconced
within a ring of trees, the best view is from Hornby Bridge where it
spans the River Wenning. Enjoy it for there is no way you can get any
closer, the surrounding land being privately owned.

During the Civil War in the 17th century, the castle was heavily fortified by Royalist troops and all assaults by the parliamentary forces were
repulsed with vigour. According to reports of the day, 'unscaleable
precipices' defended the eastern approaches of the steadfast redoubt. In

consequence, this flank was left unmanned, all available soldiers being concentrated at the vulnerable side.

Colonel Assheton was in command of the Roundhead besiegers. At a loss as to how the castle could be taken, a local sympathiser who knew of a secret way up the steep buttress approached him. A cunning plan was duly hatched and put into operation. Whilst Assheton led a distracting frontal assault, the main force accompanied their guide up the cliff route. Too late, the Royalist garrison realised their predicament. Quickly overrun by the attacking forces, the castle was given no option but to surrender.

So relieved was Oliver Cromwell when he heard the news that such a crusty carbuncle had been lanced, he gave orders that 'the Castle of Hornby be forthwith so defaced, or demolished, that the enemy may be prevented from making any further use thereof.' Its days of resistance to the new government were well and truly numbered.

The Walk

Before setting out on the walk itself, take a stroll up the main street to St Margaret's Church. Unusual in design, the octagonal tower clearly has a much more ancient pedigree than the rest of the building. There was even a church on the site in Saxon times. Edward Stanley built the tower after he had been accorded the eminent title of Lord Monteagle, Knight of the Garter. This was a reward from Henry VIII following a Scottish rout at the Battle of Flodden Field in 1513.

Stanley's intention to complete the new church was unfortunately interrupted by his untimely demise in 1524. As a contemporary rhyme elicits,

'The beauteous tower and altar then appear'd
But Stanley died before the Church was rear'd.'

His remains were interred within the grounds of Hornby Priory, which stood on an elevated dais on the banks of the River Lune to the west of the village. This was intended as a temporary measure only until such time as the noble lord could be laid to rest in the church. But a royal decree thwarted this last wish. Henry ordered the dissolution of the monasteries when they refused to condone his right to a divorce. Hornby Priory was amongst those religious houses that were desecrated and destroyed. Today it has been replaced by a farm and there is no indication that a priory ever stood there.

Nor is there any evidence that Monteagle was ever re-interred within

the new church according to
the stipulations in his will
or that a monument to his
memory was erected. In-
deed, it is thought that the
ageing bones of the great
man lie somewhere beneath
the hallowed ground near
Priory Farm.

Immerse yourself in the
primeval aura that perme-
ates the atmosphere within
this ancient tower before entering the inner sanctum of
the church proper. No re-
ports of spectral apparitions
concerning Lord Monteagle
have reached my ears – so
far. But there's always a first
time.

Leave the church and re-
turn to the bridge, passing
through a gate and along a
narrow passage to reach the
riverside walk. Head west
along the bank of the
Wenning. At the end of an
embankment on the right,
cross a raised causeway into
the adjoining field and continue. Beyond the next
fence stile, cross open pas-

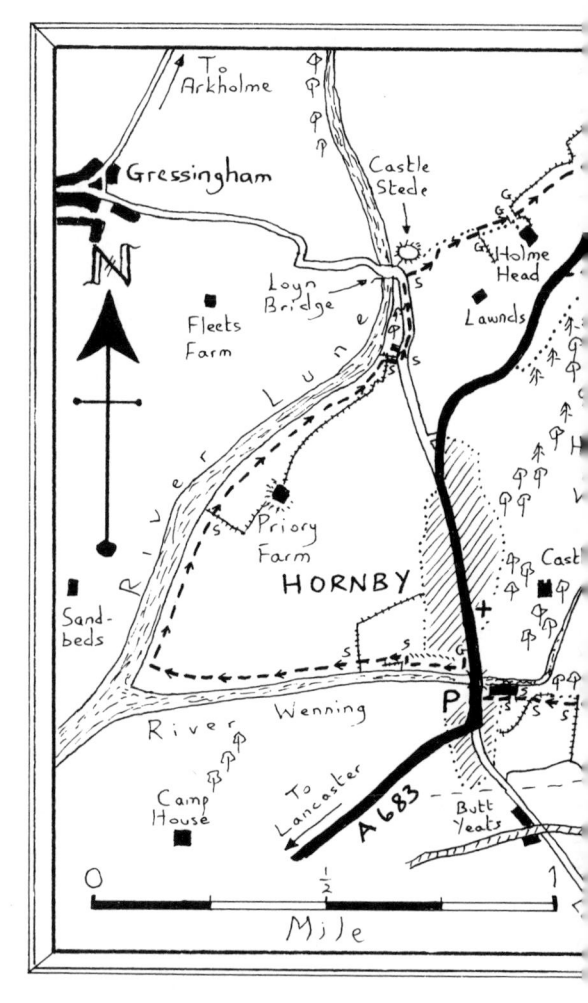

ture until the tributary merges with the Lune.

Head right upstream towards Priory Farm, perched on its elevated
stage. After the next fence stile, the untidy clutter that characterises the
farm above is soon passed. Stroll along the river terrace until forced up a
banking to join the fence on the upper level. At its far end, thick vegetation has made continuance of the right of way impassable. Go over a
stile and along a fence diversion to gain the Gressingham road. Bear left
down the road for 200 metres to a signposted stile on the right. Pass
close to a concrete lookout post adjacent to the medieval site of a motte
and bailey castle. Raised on a circular plinth to forestall an assault, it

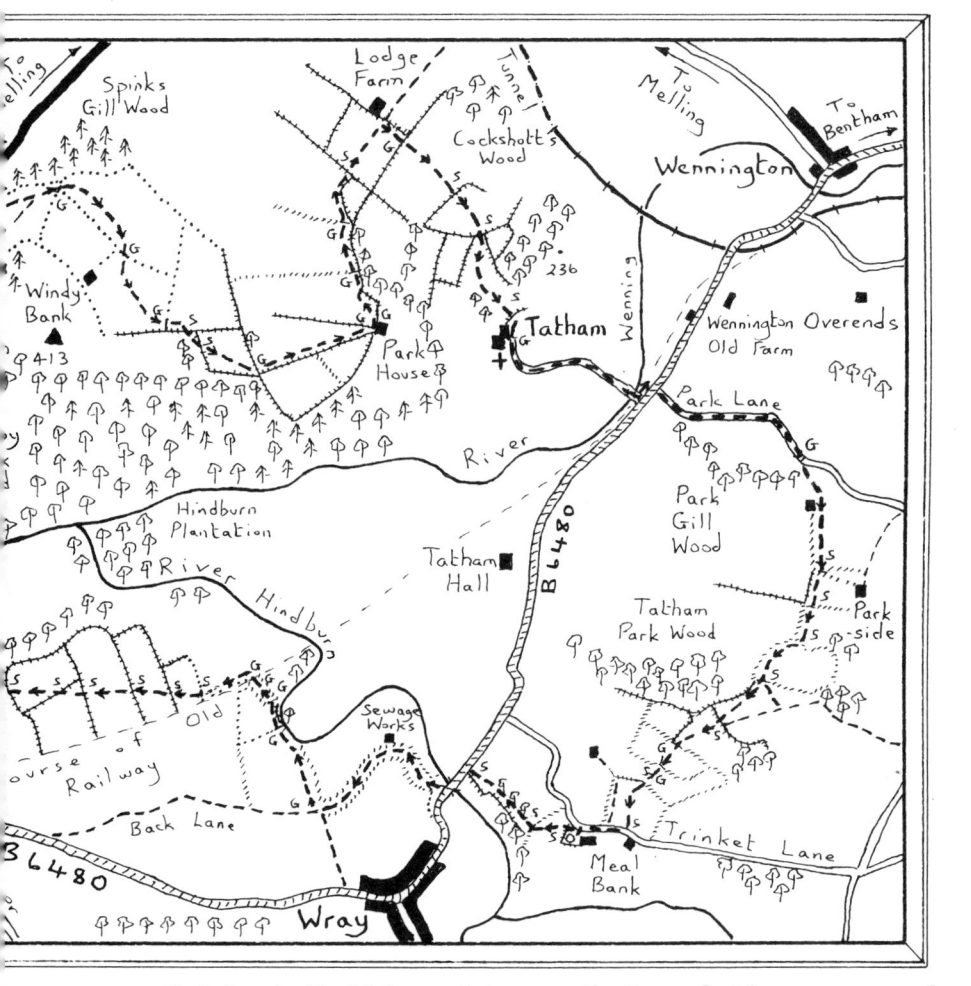

controlled the vital bridging point across the Lune that is now spanned by Loyn Bridge.

Head north-east along a wall to pass through a gate which deposits you on the opposite side for the approach to Holme Head. Another gate gives onto a major field track. Cross over into the opposite field by a stile, continuing on the same bearing along a thin trod. Aim for the far right corner a quarter mile distant. Here a stile is mounted.

Now on the busy A683, head right and back towards Hornby for no more than 200 metres, keeping well into the side as no pavement is provided. Cross over into the field opposite where a signposted gate points

St Margaret's church at Hornby with its octagonal tower

the way up the rising grass bank. The route is initially pathless but forks into a clear track as height is gained, veering into the walled enclosure of Spinks Gill Wood.

Pass through a gate at the top of the field to parallel the wall on your right. Another gate after 300 metres brings you into the adjoining field with Windy Bank Barn on the right. Make a diagonal traverse to a gate then follow a fence. Watch for a stile on the right after 100 metres which indicates a brief diversion of the right of way.

After passing through a narrow corridor of trees, cross a field track into the next field by a stile. Another diagonal traverse and you will arrive at a pair of gates hemmed in by trees. Take the left gate and head along a fence into open country slanting down towards Park House. Pass through two gates this side of the farm to gain the clear track heading north to Lodge Farm.

Accompany this route alongside a wooded stream and through two more gates until the track fades. Keep the fence on your right until a stile is reached. After this a direct walk up a gentle cant will bring you to the farm. Do not enter the environs of Lodge Farm but head right down the side of the field to a gate at the bottom.

Maintain a south-easterly course over a grassy rise before dropping down over two stiled fences, the gradient steepening as Rectory Wood is passed on the left. At the bottom, circle right and go through a gate to gain the metalled access road serving Tatham. No more than a cluster of houses and a church, the tiny hamlet is soon left behind as the lane is followed down to the Bentham road.

Turn left then right after 50 metres to follow Park Lane as it climbs out of the Wenning Valley. Beyond a road gate, keep ahead along a rough track leaning right past an isolated cottage. Head south to the top of the field and mount a stile then drop down the far side of the hill. Beyond the second stile, the hedge fans right. At the far edge of this field, cross the stile then leave the fence to cross the next field aiming for the mid-point of the fence opposite. A gentle climb takes you to a gate at the far left corner and then over the next field to yet another gate.

After crossing a stile conveniently placed to protect one's extremities from a shocking fence contact, aim for the right of Meal Bank on Trinket Lane. Head right along here for 100 metres to a farm of the same name on the left. Immediately through the main gate, bear right to enter a field abutting a blue slurry tank.

Fork half left to meet the opposite hedge and a stile after 100 metres. Follow a line of intermittent trees and go down a steep incline to rejoin the Bentham road. Head left over the bridge crossing the River Hindburn. There is no need to continue along the road into the peerless village of Wray, unless of course you arrive on May Day. Once headline news due to flooding when the River Roeburn burst its banks, it now hosts a unique annual event in company with an entourage of scarecrows.

At any other time, drop down right to take the hedged corridor which circles left behind the village as far as a gate located 200 metres beyond a sewage works. Head right down a track hedged on the right to reach the tree-girt fringe of the river. After passing through a gate, enter a hedged passage after another gate to cross the abandoned railway track. At the far side, bend left alongside a wall.

Cross a stile at the end, sticking with the wall for a further 50 metres before forking half right over to a hedge. As you cross the flat valley pastures take note of the crenellated tower of Hornby Castle poking nonchalantly above the protective scarf of trees. Maintain a due westerly bearing over three more fence stiles to arrive at the edge of a wood.

A short flight of stone steps leads to a stile and you then accompany a wall up a steepening slope. Cross a fence stile above then continue to another giving access to the wood. Take care on the tortuous path as there is a danger of slipping on the acclivitous gradient. At the far side, cross a small field to enter a farmyard by another stile then stroll along to the main road in Hornby. Immediately opposite is the car park.

Walk 7. Melling

A Trio of Surprises

Mystery: Melling Hall GR 598713

Distance: 5 miles

Total Height Climbed: 450 feet (137 metres)

Nearest Shops: Hornby

Start and Finish: Turn right off the A683 by the Melling Hall Hotel and park on Gillison Close which is the first on the left.

Maps: Ordnance Survey 1:25 000 Pathfinder 637, Burton-in-Kendal and Caton; OS Pathfinder 628, Kirkby Lonsdale and Barbon; OS Outdoor Leisure 2, Yorkshire Dales - Southern & Western areas.

One of numerous villages lining the broad sweep of the Lune Valley, Melling straddles the main road and evokes a poignant nostalgia for a more gentrified age when the horse-drawn mail coach announced its arrival with a fanfare on the post-horn, and cattle were driven to market along the main thoroughfare. Today, cottages of dressed sandstone weathered to a rustic hue would most certainly assure Melling of a place in the elite ranking of villages were it not for the busy main road. Slicing through the once calm serenity of this rural enclave, the settlement has been effectively dissected.

Approaching Melling Hall from the direction of Lancaster the road constricts appreciably, forcing traffic to slow at the bend. It is indeed a miracle that more accidents have not occurred with cars ending up in the lounge bar. Not the most auspicious method of reserving a table for dinner. At one time Melling provided an important East-West staging post with Arkholme, which was reached by means of a ferry service across the narrowing Lune. A ford is still evident although not used now, the nearest feasible crossing point being at the Loyn Bridge two miles downstream.

Most of the river crossings in the Middle Ages had defensive sites to protect travellers as well as locals from the unwelcome attentions of scurvy brigands that roamed the countryside. Melling was no exception

Melling, where a secret passage connects the hall to the church

with a motte fortification still discernible behind the village church in addition to the one on the Arkholme shore.

Solid and resolute, an indefatigable symbol of Old England, the church of St Wilfrid has enjoyed a chequered history stretching back to the 14th century. With regard to our particular interest, its most significant feature is the underground passage that connects with Melling Hall. Now blocked for safety reasons, its original purpose remains a secret although an escape route for defiant Catholic priests and their followers during the Reformation of the 16th century seems likely. The Darlington family originally owned the hall and its Georgian façade has clearly been extended at various intervals.

During the First World War, Lady Darlington did much to alleviate the suffering of troops wounded on the Western front. The hall was transformed into a convalescent home and was in such great demand that another was opened further along the main street.

It was not until some years later that the first intimation of a ghostly presence was reported in one of the guest rooms after the building had become a hotel. A lady dressed in purple was seen combing her hair in front of the dressing table mirror. When the landlady narrated this bizarre happening to an old villager, she was informed that Lady Darlington frequently wore a gown of just such a colour. Nobody who spends a night in the hall should walk in fear of a spectre that had clearly undertaken such munificent works for the benefit of the wider community.

Another weird and wonderful appearance concerns a little man who is said to jump about on the beds in a state of fervid excitement. Only 3ft tall, with a triangular face and pointed nose, his legs have been reversed with the knees at the rear. Whomsoever admits to have been heckled by this breezy leprechaun has doubtless been exercising his arm in the bar downstairs. Either that or it is my leg that is being pulled.

Last of the trio on offer at Melling Hall is a dog that is often to be heard padding softly about in the upper rooms. Investigation has predictably revealed nothing, not even the proverbial church mouse. Perhaps both had made use of the secret passage – endeavouring to fool us all!

The Walk

Take a close look at the hall as you return from the parking spot (Gillison Close) to the main road and turn right down towards the railway bridge. After 100 metres bear left along a broad track, hedged for much of its course. Veering towards the embankment, turn sharp right beyond 'Dunroamin' to pass under the railway bridge and continue along the track until it once again swings sharply to the right. At this point, go through the gate and maintain a northerly direction along a slightly raised embankment. In the days when the River Lune had divided, this acted as a flood control barrier. An island was formed over which two viaducts conveyed the newly built railway to Leeds. Today, an elongated trench containing a few finger tarns is all that remains of the Old Lune.

Mount a stile at the end and swing right along the tributary River Greta that merges with the Lune. Follow this river round to Greta Bridge where a flight of stone steps will bring you onto the main road. Bear right and cross over to take a constricted field access point down some steps located immediately beyond the old toll-cottage.

Head south across the field, nudging the old wall on the river bend and aiming for the mid-point along a line of conifers. Getting closer, a fence can be seen with a stile. Cross this and make your way up the pinched corridor to join the main street of Wrayton village. Removed from the hassle and noise of through traffic, here is a location which residents of Melling's main street would clearly covet.

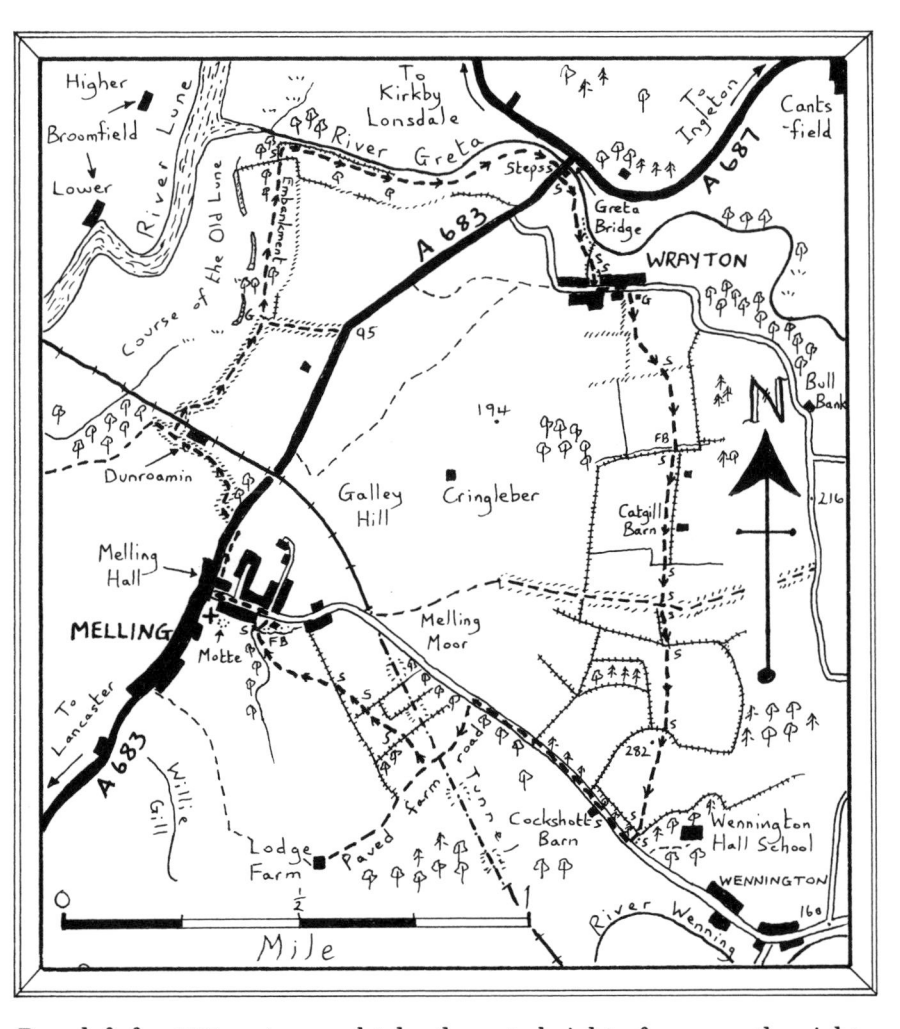

Bear left for 100 metres and take the gated right of way on the right. From here on our route is pathless but easy to follow. Initially, it passes a free-range egg factory that impoverished battery hens can only dream about. At a kink in the hedge halfway up the steepening grass bank, slant half left over the crest of the hill to mount a hedge stile in a shallow depression. Continue south over the next rise in this undulating, roller-coaster terrain then go down to a narrow plank bridge. A stile on the far side of a stream is built into the sole remaining relic of drystone walling to be found in the vicinity.

Shoot up the facing slope alongside the fence on your left, passing by two barns prior to reaching the next stile. Drop down to cross a hedged track with a stile at either side. Continue south along a recently erected fence and so to the end of the field. After negotiating this stile, make a gradual ascent of Hall Bank, keeping parallel with the fence on your right.

Just beyond the next stile, slide over the brow and descend the long grassy flank, keeping right of the gothic mansion that emerges from a sylvan dish below. The days of Wennington Hall's glory, when stately carriages drew up before its august portals, have long since faded into history. Today it serves a more immediate purpose as a special school for pupils with behavioural and learning problems.

At the bottom, cross a stile at the edge of a thin collar of trees and follow a wall to arrive at Lodge Lane. Lean right for half a mile until the access road serving Lodge Farm is reached on the left. Turn up this paved right of way for no more than 200 metres, until you are exactly above the Melling railway tunnel.

The next question that might well arise relates to the identification of this precise location. No problem. When the tunnel was first excavated, four ventilation shafts were sunk enabling smoke to dissipate. The road passes between two of these mounds which were capped when diesel superseded steam. Once in line with them, head right across an open stretch of grass, aiming for the right corner of an elliptical copse of trees.

Mount a stile to make your way down the gently shelving north-facing slope. It is in contrast to the steeply canting gradient on the far side of the Lune Valley. Head north-west to climb a fence stile at the far side of the field before veering left to cross another. Maintain a straight course down the sloping field as the outer limits of Melling village are approached.

Home in to meet a tree-lined cutting on the left and follow it down to a footbridge concealed in a right-hand loop in the brook. Immediately across, mount a wall stile that allows ingress between the gardens of local residences. Slant right down a gravel drive to rejoin Lodge Lane.

Bear left back to Melling Hall, taking particular note of a small exhibition depicting the noble art of topiary (tree shaping for the uninitiated). Not quite to the standard renowned at Levens Hall but impressive nonetheless.

Walk 8. Cowan Bridge

In Step with Jane Eyre

Mysteries: The Old School GR 634766;
Tunstall Church GR 614739

Distance: 6 miles

Total Height Climbed: Nil

Nearest Shops: Cowan Bridge

Start and Finish: Park on the village hall car park located immediately behind the post office after turning up the road to Leck. A donation is requested.

Maps: Ordnance Survey 1:25 000 Pathfinder 625, Kirkby Lonsdale and Barbon; OS Outdoor Leisure 2, Yorkshire Dales - Southern & Western areas.

Generally associated with the grim Yorkshire moors above Keighley, it may come as a surprise to many that the tiny village of Cowan Bridge has played a significant role in the Brontë saga. It was here in the early years of the 19th century that the famous sisters went to school, and where the classic 'Jane Eyre' was born. At that time, the strict and austere Reverend Carus Wilson ruled a newly opened school for the daughters of impoverished clergy with an iron hand. Try to block out the constant hum of traffic along this busy highway as you walk back towards Kirkby Lonsdale and cast your imagination back to the pre-Victorian era. Little has changed in Cowan Bridge since that time. The school is now a private residence although its aspirations are still continued at Casterton Girls School further up the Lune Valley.

Take extra care when crossing the road. It has now become a favoured route for the motorcycle fraternity who regularly converge on Devil's Bridge at Kirkby Lonsdale. Yet, even when the Brontës arrived from Haworth in 1824 the road must have been well used, conveying all manner of goods between the heartland of industrial Yorkshire and the North.

A plaque fixed to the gable-end of what became universally recognised as Lowood School informs us that four of the five sisters attended.

The untimely demise of Maria and Elizabeth from consumption, no doubt exacerbated by the harsh conditions at the school, led Patrick Brontë to remove his other daughters for their own safety. Much of what Jane Eyre suffered at the hands of the tyrannical regime was drawn from Charlotte's own memory.

The Walk

Our walk begins along the footpath at the side of the old school and accompanies the chattering surge of Leck Beck downstream to join the River Lune at Burrow. Follow the route taken by the children of the school whatever the weather to the church at Tunstall. To experience the true nature of how this walk affected the girls, try it in the depths of winter with a blizzard howling in your ear.

The wall on the right soon gives way to a fence where the collapsed pathway has been restored and the banking reinforced. Continue along to the access serving High Gale, here paved, until the footbridge spanning the beck is reached. Here it was that the forlorn procession of little girls crossed to take the more direct route along Woodman Lane. More interesting for us, however, is to carry on until a fence stile on the right gives access to the field path.

Bear left, across the field, to a gate at the edge of Low Gale. Then make a diagonal crossing to a ladder stile adjoining Eller Beck, which is then crossed by a slab footbridge. Keep ahead alongside a fence until it veers away to the left. Drop down a gentle slope to parallel a line of trees on the right up to a wall.

Mount the stile and follow the edge of an escarpment on the right to merge with a walled field track near a large barn. Pass through a gate and go along the track to another gate close to Burrow Hall. The track now bends to the right, passing Johnson house and going over the paved farmyard. Stick with the track to arrive at the A683 soon after. Bear left towards Nether Burrow along this well-used road. Keep to the grass verge as there is no pavement. Immediately before the Highwayman Inn, a lane branching left can be taken if the extra distance to visit Tunstall Church lies outside your allotted time schedule. Fans of *Jane Eyre* will have no such hesitation, surging ahead for another 100 metres along the main road, go past the inn and through a gate into the fields.

Head due south towards the distant tower of the church, veering away from the road and aiming for the mid-point of a fence and the next gate. Maintain a straight line to reach the wall corner at the far side of

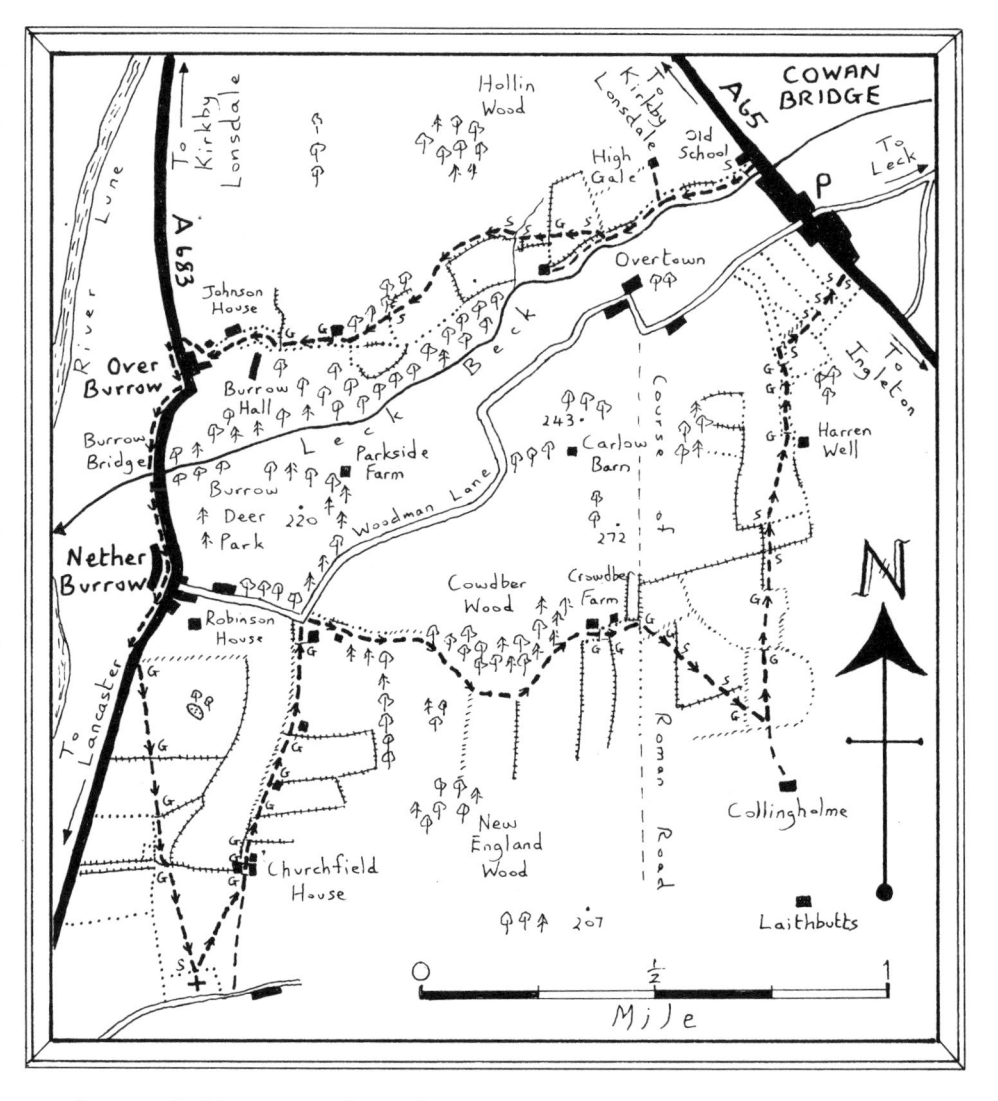

the next field, passing through a third gate to follow the wall and then a fence which tapers in towards the corner. There is a gate at the end of the fence. Cross the last field to its far side and a wall stile giving entry to the churchyard. Well-tended graveyards complement the old church of St John the Baptist, which has tolled its bell for worship since the 13th century. A cleric known only as Richard was the first-known incumbent, according to the records.

Tunstall church, which Charlotte Brontë attended

Especially interesting for us is the inclusion of the Reverend Carus Wilson who brought the young ladies of Cowan Bridge School on the five-mile round trip every Sunday. Neither blinding snow nor driving rain was sufficient reason for him to deny his captive flock their regular diatribe from his pulpit. He even produced a journal in which the scourging of body and soul was an essential requirement of religious upbringing. Known as *The Children's Friend*, it paid little regard to any form of love or compassion, a sympathetic and congenial understanding of young minds being far removed from its stark message.

A small room located above the entrance porch to the church is where the girls ate their meagre lunch after the service and prior to the return journey. Accompany their memory at least for the first mile by stepping back into the field behind the church and slanting half right across to Churchfield House. Take the left-hand gate, which sports a wheeled design, to go through the farmyard. At the top end, go along a narrow passage between a barn and old tyre dump to reach the field gate at the rear. Keep the fence/hedge on your left as you go through two more gates up to Kirkriggs Barn. Stick with the hedge along the edge of the next field (gated at both ends) to arrive at a modern farm building.

The track is much clearer as it conveys us to a sharp bend in Woodman Lane with a smart, new, stone house on the corner. Purists and Brontë fans may wish to stay with the original route along the lane to Overtown. Good luck to them as the rest heave right along a rough access track that swings between banks of mixed woodland and low grassy knolls to reach Cowdber Farm.

Pass right of the renovated outbuildings through a gate then follow a wall adjacent to the old farm itself. Lean in towards the left edge of the field to pass through a gate.

Here the original course of the Roman road can be made out forging across the countryside in a North/South orientation. Extraordinary road builders of considerable skill, the Roman engineers made highways to last and rarely deviated from a direct line. In consequence, the marching legions were able to cover vast distances at a rapid pace – just one of the many reasons why their empire once covered most of the known world.

Maintain a south-easterly course over a newly erected fence and stile followed by another after 200 metres to cut off a field corner and so emerge through a gate. Joining the right of way between Cowan Bridge and Collingholme, turn north up the sloping field to pass through a gate in the next hedge. Keep onward to another gate close to a hedged corner running over the crest of the hill.

As you stroll along the right side of the hedge, glance right to where the skyline is dominated by the table top of mighty Ingleborough. I wonder if the Brontë sisters ever made it to the summit.

Go over a stile then another in a wall to arrive at the edge of a large field. Fork half right, aiming for the dilapidated structure known as Harren Well. Just beyond, a gate marks the start of a rough, walled lane. The lane is heavily overgrown though still walkable (machetes being an optional extra). It has clearly not been used by farm traffic for many years.

Make your way along the narrow passage for 300 metres, opening two gates en route. Just past the second, watch for a wall stile on the right. Enter the field and walk along its edge to a wall and stile. From here, two more walls with accompanying stiles must be negotiated to bring you to the main road.

Head left back towards downtown Cowan Bridge. Hopefully you will have dry feet, unlike the luckless Jane Eyre. She related that on the weekly church visit in winter, she and her colleagues had, 'no boots, the snow got into our shoes, and melted there: our un-gloved hands became numbed and covered with chilblains, as were our feet.'

Walk 9. Thurnham Hall

A Ghostly Threesome

Mystery: Thurnham Hall GR 464546

Distance: 5½ miles

Total Height Climbed: 100 feet (30 metres)

Nearest Shops: Galgate

Start and Finish: Park on the gravel lay-by alongside a telephone box 200 metres south of Upper Thurnham, on the A588 road to Cockerham.

Map: Ordnance Survey 1:25 000 Pathfinder 659, Galgate and Dolphinholme

---

On the day I undertook this particular walk it had been my intention to stand on the Roof of Lancashire. A leaden sky skulking in from the west soon unleashed a torrential downpour that proceeded to hammer the earth into submission. This walk was nonetheless enjoyable and an ideal replacement, even though I saw no evidence of the Thurnham spectres. They must have been sheltering from the boisterous elements.

Of 13th-century origin, Thurnham Hall was occupied by the re-nowned Dalton Family for 450 years. It fell into disrepair when they stumbled upon hard times. In 1973 it was acquired by Stanley Crabtree of Rochdale who has restored the property to its former glory through an extensive programme of refurbishment. The task has been accomplished with panache and the owner has managed to retain the authentic flavour of the original house while transforming it into a time-share complex.

Oldest of the ghosts known to haunt the corridors of Thurnham Hall is a Cavalier from the period of the Civil War. Thought to be a certain Colonel Thomas Dalton, he has been observed dashing along the upper landing of the house. For what reason and whether he was astride a snorting charger at the time has never been revealed.

Elizabeth Dalton was the Lady of the House during the middle years of the 19th century and it was she who added the distinctive chapel extension in 1845. Her ghost has been sighted walking through her old bedroom clad in a green dress on numerous occasions. It seems fairly certain that this is the enigmatic young woman who was witnessed in recent years 'floating' across the lawn in front of the chapel. Said to be wearing garments like those of a nun, she then simply vanished into the trees.

Last of the trio, a somewhat impish boggart is said to have scattered the sticks laid in the fireplace. Snatching bedclothes off slumbering guests is also thought to be one of his tricks. Jessica Lofthouse, the eminent Lancashire folklore expert, said that a boggart 'could be sly, full of mischievous pranks, his nuisance value high. But he rarely did serious harm and was often helpful in the "good brownie" family tradition that he was usually tolerated.' As 'made' fires and bedding have largely given way to central heating and duvets; it would appear that this particular boggart has been inactive for some considerable time. Maybe the intense human activity surrounding the hall today might encourage the spirited little rascal to resume his antics.

The old chapel at Thurnham Hall

The Walk

Our walk begins by walking up the road to the entrance to Thurnham Hall. Here the last of the Daltons, Miss Alzira Eloise, lived in a cottage until her death in 1983. Walk up the access track serving the hall and consider its unique heritage as you pass to the right, following the rough track round to the local church. Staunchly Catholic in their religious leanings, the Dalton family chapel was replaced in 1848 by the 'inspired' building that now beckons the faithful of the parish. Isolated amidst the sprawling trees of Thurnham estate, one can only speculate as to why such a grandiose structure was created in this outlandish position. Could it be that Catholicism was still not fully accepted by the majority of citizens?

Continue along the clear track that terminates at Cock Hall Farm. Bear left at the first barn to cross a field on a track that cuts through a narrow strip of woodland. Pass through a gap and go over a thin stream, forging ahead along a grass trail. Ignore a path forking left towards the Glasson Dock branch of the Lancashire Canal. After a further 100 metres, veer sharp right to a stile and then left along a hedge to a fence.

Step over this and stroll on as far as a gate in the hedge on the left. Here lean right, soon bending left towards extensive woodland ahead. Mount a waymarked stile alongside a gate into dense woodland and make your way along the fringe until another stile is reached, there to exit from the wood. Walk along its edge until a gate and stile are reached, near some sheds.

Re-enter the wood. It is soon left as the path climbs a slight gradient to Home Farm. Cross straight over the access road and proceed along a narrow, rather overgrown passage created at the left side of the field for through movement. It is far easier to stroll along the outside of the strip-steel fence even though this is not strictly on the right of way.

At the terminus of this constricting alley, climb over a fence hurdle (no stile provided) and aim half left towards the Lancaster Canal. Keep above the valley bottom, which appears to be on the marshy side judging by its reedy appearance. Although pathless, you should experience no difficulty slanting in to reach the canal at a unique double bridge. Two for the price of one, but for what purpose?

Amble along the wooded fringe of the canal to pass through a wall gap and over Junction Bridge. A lock marks the convergence of the Glasson branch with the main canal. Head north along the towpath, passing under two bridges. Look for a hidden stile in the hedge near to the limit of Galgate's built-up suburb.

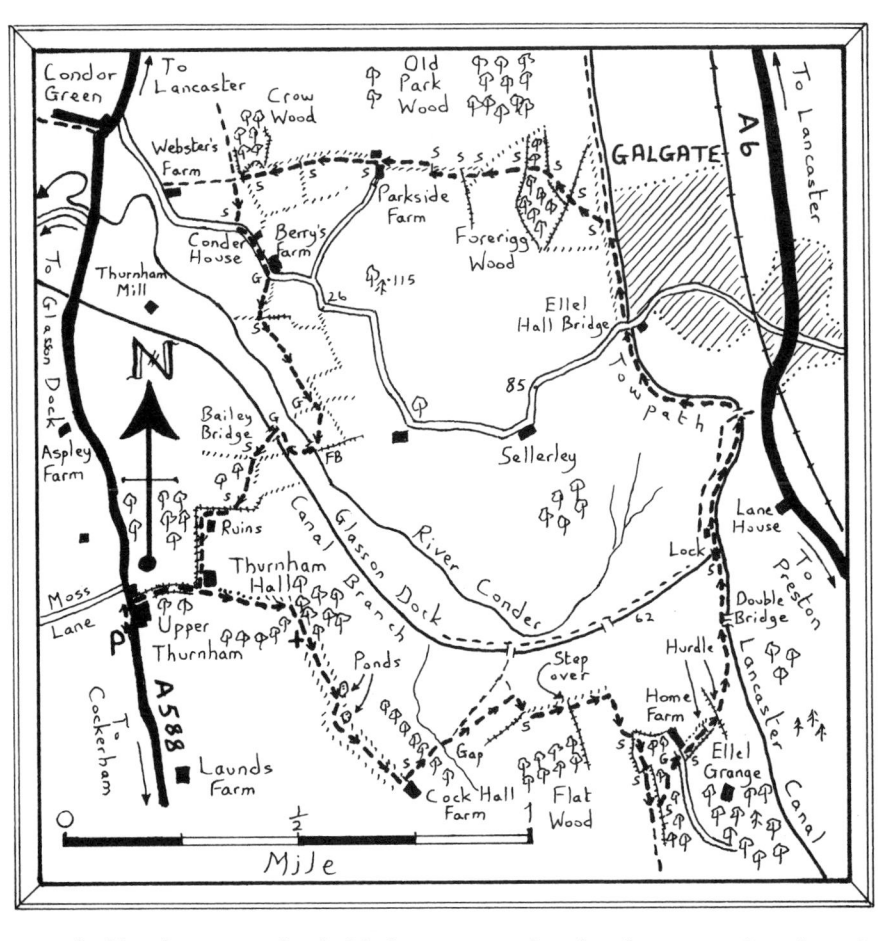

Lean half right across the field along a raised embankment to the edge of
Forerigg Wood. Over a fence stile, watch for a concealed stile giving access to the wood. Soon after emerging at the far side, aim directly for a
large tree prodding the sky above the rising hillock in front. Drop down
the far side over two stiles then accompany a hedge on your right. Top-
ping another gentle uplift, swap to the far side by a stile and continue
down to Parkside Farm. At the opposite side of the yard, pass through a
gap stile and continue along the hedge down to Crow Wood. Two hedge
stiles will bring you to an indistinct footpath crossroads at the western
limit of the wood.

Head left across the field, keeping to the right of Conder House,
which is the distinctive white building ahead. Join the back lane, turn-

ing left towards Galgate for 200 metres to pass through a gate opposite Berry's Farm. Walk along the hedge to a stile then slant half left towards a distinct corner.

Stroll along the hedge to a gate then make a diagonal beeline to the far right corner to cross the River Conder on a substantial footbridge. At its far side, continue ahead to meet the Lancaster Canal swerving right to Bailey Bridge – which is also crossed. A faint path in the grass then leads you to a stile in the thorny hedge.

Follow a little-used and sunken trackway with a scattering of trees on either side. At the end, cross open ground to the fence enclosing Thurnham Hall and go over a stile. Bear right for 100 metres then left past a cluster of decaying outbuildings. Pass the imposing façade of the hall with its battlemented fringe and head right down the access track back to the A588.

Walk 10. Cockerham

The Devil's Stride

Mysteries: The Three Wishes GR 463519;
Cockersand Abbey GR 427537

Distance: 7½ miles

Total Height Climbed: Insignificant

Nearest Shops: Cockerham

Start and Finish: Park on the forecourt of Cockerham village hall.
This is 200 metres south of the Manor Inn on the B5272.

Map: Ordnance Survey 1:25 000 Pathfinder 659, Galgate and
Dolphinholme

With a name meaning 'a homestead adjacent to the River Cocker', the
original site of Cockerham was much closer to the river's mouth than is
the case today. Excessive flooding later saw the village being abandoned in favour the current site above the moss land. St Michael's
Church, once at the heart of village life, now stands isolated amid grassy
fields a quarter of a mile to the west. Like a child with no one to play
with, it presents a rather forlorn aura of rejection.

In suitable conditions the sun can pick out the street plan of old
Cockerham, which was burnt down in the 17th century. Today's village, quiet and somewhat prosaic, bears little relation to the lively enclave of old. Horse racing, bowling and cockfighting are just some of the
ribald activities regularly enjoyed by the residents.

Our first visit on this outing involves the easy walk down to the
church, at the end of a metalled access road on the right of the parish
hall. Surrounded by a drystone wall, rare indeed in this locality, the village school was at one time situated in the north-east corner. The
schoolmaster was highly regarded for the breadth of his knowledge,
such esteem resulting in him being called upon to rid the village of a
particularly unwelcome visitor.

Having been bested in the town of Clitheroe, the Devil arrived in a
foul temper and proceeded to create all manner of objectionable indig-

nities amongst the villagers. Such devilish intrigue led to the teacher being appointed as their knight-errant. Quaking with fear, as well he might when challenging Old Nick's scheming chicanery, the fellow finally raised the horned demon from his slumbers. His Satanic Majesty felt pleased that his presence had caused such trepidation amongst the populace and granted the teacher three tasks for him to perform. If they were undertaken successfully, the teacher would become his eternal slave. If not, he would leave Cockerham, never to return.

The first test presented by the wily pedagogue was for the Devil to count the number of dewdrops on the surrounding hedgerows. This he accomplished with ease, although how such a task could be proved has never been mentioned. Next was to count the stalks in a field of wheat – an equally simple feat for such as he. The final commission involved plaiting a rope of sand on the banks of the Cocker that would not lose a single strand when washed by the rising waters.

'Why do you waste my time with these witless follies,' scoffed Old Nick, setting to with relish. 'Prepare to stoke the fires of Hell.'

As the river caressed the rope of sand, the outline began to fade and had soon blended with the rest of the riverbank and was no more. 'There!' cried the teacher in undisguised mirth. 'Where is your rope of sand now?'

So incensed was the Lord of Darkness that he stamped over Pilling Moss and was never heard from again in this locality. The distance from Cockerham to Pilling is seven miles and has become known as 'The Devil's Stride'. Here is a brief extract from an ode penned by a literary wit of the day and which might stimulate the chuckle muscles.

> *'Now the poor fellow was a pitiful case.*
> *As plain might be seen from the long length of face.*
> *"Now make me, dear sir, a rope of your sand,*
> *Which will bear washing and not lose a strand."*
> *The devil and mate then went down to the strand,*
> *In a jiffy they twisted a fine rope of sand,*
> *And dragged it along with them over the land;*
> *But when they brought the rope to be washed,*
> *To atoms it went all – the rope was all smashed.*
> *The devil was foiled, wrath, and gave him a shaking;*
> *Up he flew to the steeple – his frame all a-quaking.*
> *With one horrid frig – his mind very unwilling,*
> *He strode to the brig o'er Broadfleet at Pilling.*

The Walk

Keep to the right of the church to emerge on a path at the far side that links with the main road. Turn left for 200 metres then take the signposted path on the right. Follow a fenced dyke over two footbridges, aiming north-west towards a small copse of trees half a mile distant.

Beyond the next stile, the caravan headquarters of the Black Knights' Parachute Club hoves into view on the left. On most fine weekends in summer, the daring exploits of these paladins of the sky can be enjoyed hereabouts. I still recall with mixed feelings a day's course undertaken at the club followed by two controlled descents from the Cessna turbo-prop aircraft. Leaping out at 2500ft then gently drifting down to land unceremoniously on terra firma is both terrifying and intoxicating at the same time. Call in for details if it stirs the blood and sets your skin a-tingling!

Less daring souls should head straight over to a group of trees and cross the footbridge and stile. You reach a field corner then the main embankment where Cockerham Marsh opens out before you. Take a right along the top of this flood control barrier to a lone house, there to join the Parachute Club access road.

Cross to the far side of Hillam Lane and the continuation of the embankment, which runs arrow straight heading due west towards Bank End half a mile away. Circle round to the left of the farm buildings and caravan park to join a path accompanying the sea wall along to the next group of caravans at Bank Houses.

Keep to the seaward side along the metalled service road and through a stile at the far end. The path swings to the north following the edge of the shoreline with a fence on your right. Beyond the next stile, flat grass pastures open out. Stick to the rim of the reinforced boulder clay, noting the sea's awesome power where breeches have occurred.

Ahead, the conical roof of what remains of Cockersands Abbey thrusts its cross at the louring sky. On a fine day it offers an idyllic locale to wile away the afternoon in silent contemplation. But it is a bleak and lonely spot when biting westerlies pile in off the Irish Sea, a feature that no doubt contributed to the abbey being established here.

All that remains of what was the third richest house in Lancashire at the time of the Reformation is one side of the octagonal chapter house, plus oddments of walling. The Daltons used the obvious later addition as a family mausoleum until it was acquired by English Heritage. Originally founded as a hermitage, it later became a hospital for retired monks prior to being adopted by the Premonstratensian Order back in

1190. Known as White Canons on account of their distinctive woollen habits, the order took its name from the mother abbey at Premontre in France, the best surviving example in northern England being at Shap in Cumbria.

It was later dissolved by Henry VIII and the rich array of contents removed. A wooden depiction of Christ known as a rood was, however, concealed by the villagers. Mary I later allowed it to be restored. Unfortunately, during the intervening years the carving had decayed. A new image was commissioned, but upon completion the village elders refused to pay the carpenter's fee. Their reason was that the new effigy was hideous and likely to frighten the children. Summoned before the Mayor of Lancaster, the verdict was that the carpenter had done his best and therefore the churchwardens must pay up.

The carpenter had the last word on the subject, commenting that 'if the parishioners did not like their God, they could put a pair of horns on him and he would make a capital devil'. In such insular comunities, it is unlikely that the fellow was able to acquire much work after this episode and he no doubt moved away, taking his tools with him.

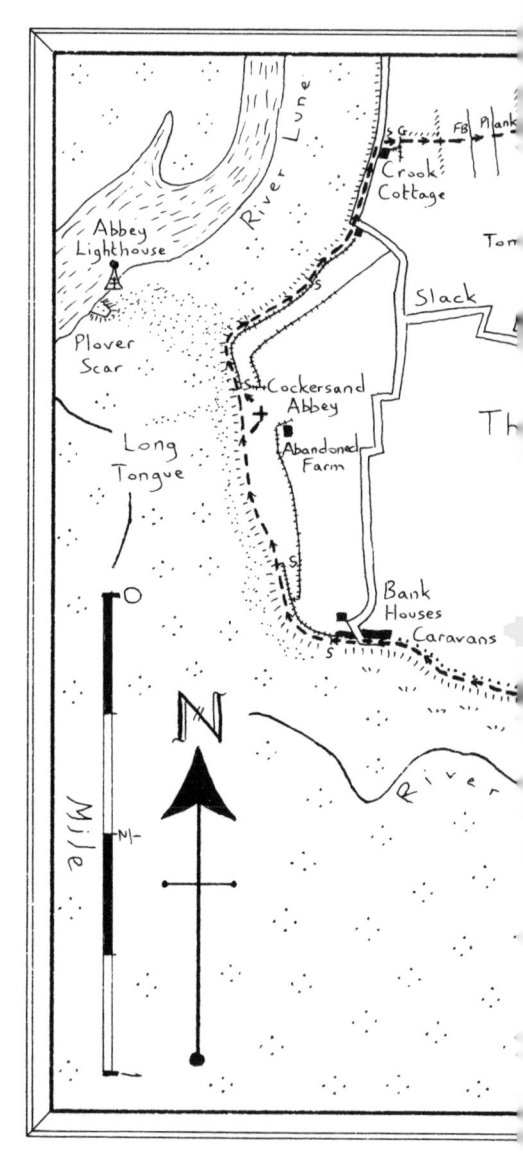

Now that Thurnham Moss has been drained and flood barriers erected, it is difficult to imagine how austere this situation was in medieval times. The oldest settlements were built on 'clay islands' that rose

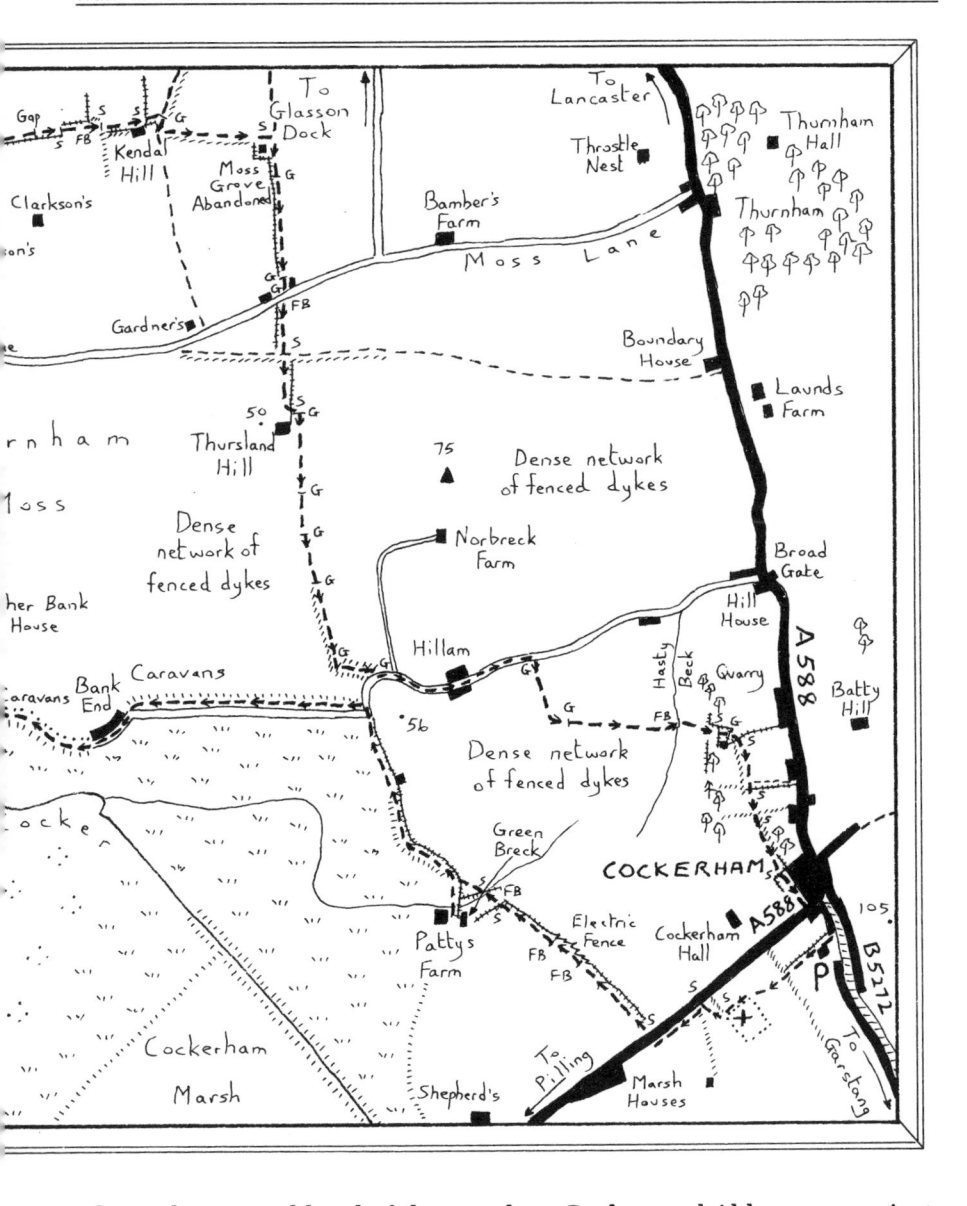

above the general level of the marshes. Cockersand Abbey was on just such an excrescence, along with those farms on Thursland Hill and Norbreck. Few more isolated spots could have been chosen – which to the White Canons, I am sure, would have been a distinct advantage.

A bleak and lonely setting for Cockersands Abbey

Continue north through a stile to round Plover Hill. Across the Lune estuary lies the old port of Sunderland which still gets cut off by the incoming tide on a regular basis (See Walk 4). Pass the end of Slack Lane with Abbey Lighthouse Cottage on the right. Another 200 metres will bring you to Crook Cottage. Lean right over a stile and go down the side of the cottage to a gate that gives onto a hedged field. Head east in a direct line towards Kendal Hill Farm. Numerous fenced dykes are accompanied on the way. Keep left of the farm buildings as you follow a fence to gain the access road close to a bungalow.

Stroll down the road for 100 metres, cutting right through a gate before continuing east along the right-hand side of a hedge. Passing through a gate you will arrive at a fence stile adjoining the abandoned farm of Moss Grove. Bear right to head south on a straight course to reach Moss Lane. On the far side, a stile and footbridge allow continued progress towards the distinctive oasis of Thursland Hill.

Arriving at a footpath crossroads, keep ahead over a stile. Avoid the settlement by crossing a stile and gate together, circling left and so maintaining a southerly direction to Hillam Lane. On your left is a consummate example of how early settlers took advantage of the 'clay islands' to keep their feet dry during the rainy season. In this area that's all through the year.

The final section of the path swings sharply to the left and through two gates to arrive at Hillam Lane. Bear left past Hillam Farm to take a footpath 200 metres beyond on the right. Make sure to use the first gate and then to go along the clear field track.

Watch out for the first gate encountered on the far side of the fenced dyke. A haunting yet melodic refrain is picked out on this rustic instrument when the wind decides to comply. Listen carefully. Could it be the Magic Flute perhaps?

The path swings to the left through a gate and then crosses Hasty Beck via a substantial footbridge. Lean half right towards an isolated building of recent construction. The right of way passes round to the left of a garden, emerging by a stile on to the rough access track. Stick with this until it veers left to the main road. Cross a stile and continue ahead for 100 metres, when another is negotiated. Mount a brief rise with a hedge on the left. Soon you will arrive at a fence that forms the limit of Cockerham's housing development. A grassy enclosure gives way to a track passing a craft workshop and so down to the main road. Bear left then right past the Manor Inn for a return to the parish hall.

Folklore and a strong historical tradition coalesce in syncopated fusion around Cockerham, a rhythmic blend that complements this rural backwater. Challenged and rebuffed by his erstwhile foe, the Devil, clad in the guise of a defiant sea, has been effectively tamed by flood barriers – for the present at least.

Walk 11. Jubilee Tower

A Celebration in Stone

Mysteries: Jubilee Tower GR 542573;
Rowton Brook Farm GR 529592

Distance: 6 miles

Total Height Climbed: 900 feet (274 metres)

Nearest Shops: Lancaster

Start and Finish: A car park is provided opposite the Jubilee Tower.

Maps: Ordnance Survey 1:25 000 Outdoor Leisure 41, Forest of Bowland and Ribblesdale

---

Bleak and lonely, the squat memorial erected to celebrate the 50th anniversary of Queen Victoria's reign stands proud and aloof high on this north-west flank along the Trough of Bowland road. A resilient testament to a period in history when the populace considered it a privilege to be part of a Britain that could indeed call itself Great. Such monuments remain a poignant reminder of a time when royalty was held in high esteem for its own sake.

The castellated block, solid and unyielding, affords an impressive prospect to the west across the indented outline of Morecambe Bay towards the Lakeland hills. This is as far as most visitors get. A great pity that the majority will miss out on a walk of scenic contrasts culminating in the enviable panorama atop Clougha Pike.

Erected in 1887 under the direction of James Harrison from Hare Appletree, Jubilee Tower was placed in the hands of public ownership in 1973 to ensure its preservation. For over a century, the gaunt austerity of this imposing edifice has absorbed all that Mother Nature could dispense. It complements the barren wilderness that encompasses the Bowland fell country and the patriotic Victorian farmer could have selected no more fitting situation.

It also marks the site of a much older association with human endeavour that stretches back into the Dark Ages. When the car park

Hare Appletree Farm, where the builder of Jubilee Tower lived.

was being excavated, a 7th-century coffin hewn from a tree trunk was uncovered, complete with a preserved death shroud now on display in Lancaster Museum.

The Walk

After mounting the flight of stone steps for the obligatory view, head west down a reed-choked bank abutting the wall to Westfield House. Continue past the farm to cross a cattle grid where a wall stile on the right points the way north alongside a wall. An embankment of gargantuan boulders offers another tantalising enigma to mull over whilst strolling along to cross the next fence stile.

Beyond the wall stile at the end of this field, our route leans to the left accompanying a fenced gill. Straddle a cutting close to a line of trees and a fence stile on the far bank then head north-west across broken ground, aiming for the farming hamlet of Hare Appletree. Beyond the stile adjoining the farm, keep left of a large blue slurry tank and go along to join the farm road on the left. The old farmhouse, complete with its complement of tiny windows, harks back to an era well before that of James Harrison. Pass right of this majestic mansion to accompany the road for 200 metres until a trio of gates is reached on the left.

Take the last of these and so up a field track along a fenced corridor. Passing over the gentle dome of Middle Brow, descend the back slope to the far right corner of the field, where a back lane is joined. Head right to Quernmore Brow, then right for 50 metres before turning into the craft shop and tea rooms of Brow Top.

Bear left and take a few moments to enjoy the variety of fauna being raised in the barn. In addition to the expected woollies, llamas, peacocks and Shetland ponies co-exist in placid harmony. Pass through a gate, heading north alongside a wall. After crossing two stiles close together, lean half right across a field towards the farming complex of Rowton Brook.

Some unusual circumstances need to be contemplated as you negotiate the tortuous route through the settlement enclave. A thriving millinery industry operating here once supplied headgear for export to the West Indies via Glasson Dock. Most of the hats were destined to be worn by slaves and convicts. In return, Rowton Brook's remote situation made it ideal for storing illicit brandy smuggled in through Glasson. It was then a simple task to distribute the potent hooch along lonely trails unfrequented by the dreaded revenue men.

The 17th century brought forth the touching story concerning John Kelsall, a zealous Quaker persecuted for his faith and banished to the West Indies. When his wife died in London, two orphan boys were left in the harsh care of the Poor Law authorities. Their grandmother undertook the arduous commission of locating and bringing them back to Rowton concealed in saddlebags slung across her horse.

Clearly this is a farm of some import. Mount a stile close to the first building. Pass through a gap and turn left then immediately right again over a corner wall stile that is easily missed. Follow the wall around to cross a fence stile followed by a small footbridge spanning Rowton Brook. Continue ahead to another part of the hamlet, bearing right where a distinctive sign on the barn points the way 'To Clougha'.

Move ahead, taking the right fork through a gate. The track then swings right over Rowton Brook. Climbing the gently graded slopes alongside the brook, our route negotiates three wall stiles before gaining the open fell. Re-cross the brook and soon the rock-strewn ramparts defending the citadel of Clougha Pike are reached.

Access to the 'projecting ridge' which gives the fell its name is afforded by a prominent groove slanting up the final shift onto the rough summit plateau. The trig column is initially hidden behind a large stone shelter, but it is the visually stunning pageant that will command atten-

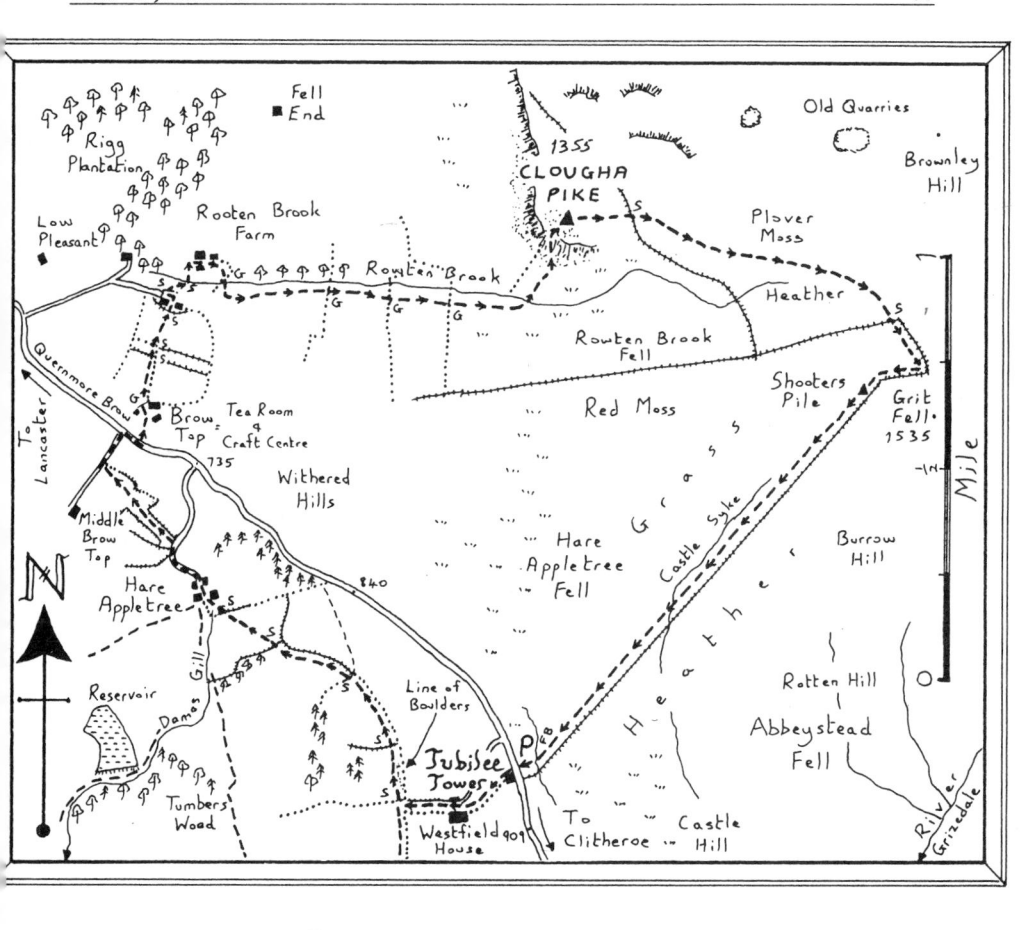

tion. Especially when a silvery tide fills the myriad coves and inlets around Morecambe Bay, the view is nothing short of breathtaking. Clichés slip off the tongue with practised ease: glorious, picturesque, spectacular, amazing. All equally applicable, and why not? The entire panoply of North Lancashire laid out in perfect symmetry and supported by the scabrous backdrop of the Lakeland Fells. Who could ask for more?

Perhaps it is appropriate for this walk that James Harrison lit a beacon on the summit as a finale to celebrate Queen Victoria's jubilee. Clougha was never regarded as an official beacon site, the last one being a celebration of Victory in Europe back in 1945.

Take lunch within the confines of the stone enclosure, which offers protection from the belligerent westerlies bustling overhead to feed the wind farm on Caton Moor. Thereafter, head off east across the plateau on a clear path. After 200 metres a fence stile is climbed as the path assumes a wide loop to the right across the barren heather moorland. Rising gradually, we soon arrive at the fence that marks the limit of the permitted area of access.

Most of the upland that encloses the Trough of Bowland has been placed out of bounds to walkers except for certain corridor routes and access zones. This has been a matter of fierce contention between ramblers and landowners for many years. A recent compromise has enabled more land to be opened up for walkers to enjoy. Hopefully, some form of permanent solution can be reached in the near future that will be acceptable to all concerned.

Cross the fence stile and follow it round to the right before the short descent to Shooters Pile. This is clearly a reference to those who make the Glorious Twelfth a day of celebration – it's certainly not for the grouse. Beyond this bulbous monolith, the arrow-straight fence marks a distinct separation betwixt heather and grass, and leads unerringly down to Jubilee Tower.

Walk 12. Garstang

Daggers Drawn

Mysteries: Greenhalgh Castle GR 501452;
Blackburn Jack GR 484430

Distance: 7½ miles

Total Height Climbed: Insignificant

Nearest Shops: Garstang

Start and Finish: Do this walk on a Sunday when free parking is available on the large council car park by the river in Garstang.

Map: Ordnance Survey 1:25 000 Outdoor Leisure 41, Forest of Bowland & Ribblesdale.

On a low knoll overlooking Gubberford Bridge to the east of Garstang lies Greenhalgh Castle, or what is left of it. Hidden by a small copse of trees, the bare ribs of this once regal pile remain largely unnoticed by visitors in the town below.

Garstang grew to prominence as a market centre of the Fylde sited at an important bridging point over the river Wyre when such facilities were vital for movement around the country. Today, the town has developed into a dormitory settlement for commuters working in Preston, Blackpool and Lancaster. During that early phase it was the Stanleys who held sway in the locality. Being ardent supporters of the victorious Henry Tudor who won his crown at the Battle of Bosworth in 1485 assured the family's prosperity. As a royal favour, Henry granted land upon which the sturdy fortress was erected.

Primarily regarded as a military stronghold, it commanded an extensive vista across the breadth of the Wyre Valley. No intrusive elements could cross Gubberford Bridge without the knowledge of the castle guards. Protected by a moat and drawbridge, the dour citadel assisted the prosperity of the Stanleys until they mistakenly backed the Royalist cause during the Civil War. Cromwell's incensed troops ripped the castle apart, the rubble being later utilised in the building of Castle Farm immediately behind the promontory. Only the ragged vestiges of a

The gaunt remains of Greenhalgh Castle

once-proud fortress are left under the watchful gaze of the attendant bovines, a gaunt shell acting as a poignant reminder of the virulent times from which it emerged.

And in keeping with the best traditions associated with all such relics, a resident ghost now haunts the ruins. The story is told concerning one of the parliamentary soldiers who was on watch along the battlements of the castle one summer's day sometime around the year 1650. Peering down from his vantage point towards Gubberford Bridge, he saw his faithless wife sauntering along the riverbank. Incapable of remaining loyal to her espoused, the errant wench had bigamously married a cavalry officer. This gullible fellow was treated in the same feckless manner. Suddenly, the distraught trooper appeared from the bushes and stabbed his wayward lover to death.

Deserting his post, the parliamentarian ran down the hill to remonstrate with his adversary. On learning that the woman was indeed something of a reckless trollop, both men proceeded to bury her where she had fallen by the riverbank. So if you chance to pass this way on some dusky August evening, don't be too perturbed should a lady in white beckon with flashing eyes. Naturally, the apparition is only likely to be perceived by male walkers.

The Walk

The castle is barely discernible from the car park in Garstang as you take the river walk, heading downstream towards Gubberford Bridge. After 200 metres, it veers to the right and joins the B6430 where you make a left over the bridge. On the far side of the River Wyre, bear left up Castle Lane. Climbing gradually, the exposed ribs of the ruin are soon reached at the apex of the access road serving Castle Farm. Recall its colourful past as you pass this ancient monument whose stonework was recycled to build the farm.

Of the two gates on the right, pass through that nearest the farm to walk alongside a hedge and through a gap at the end of the field. Cross the next field to mount a hedge stile, sticking with the fence on your right and ignoring the obvious track circling left.

Beyond a gate, keep ahead up to the next hedge stile. Then lean half left across the field towards the railway. Open the gate to bear right, heading south through two more gates which will bring you to an old stone bridge spanning the Lancaster Canal. Over the bridge, swing immediately left over a fence hurdle to gain the canal towpath once utilised by horse-drawn barges plying up and down between Kendal and Preston. Take a casual stroll along the canal, continuing south until you reach the second bridge just beyond a factory and Catterall Basin on the far bank.

This is a poignant time to recall that three succeeding generations of transport run side by side down this sector of the Wyre Valley. Leave the canal at this point to head west down a hedged track. Arriving at Sturzaker House, bear right until you reach the first gate on the left. Pass through this and follow the hedge on your right over three fields to a short constricted passage stiled at each end.

Cross the road (B6430) and Calder Bridge to take the riverside path by some playing fields. Stick with the River Calder past its junction with the Wyre until the path merges with a works access track. Head right past more commercial sites to reach the A6. Cross over and walk back towards the Blackpool road, taking the first left to back up along the original course of the main road. Make a right along a path signposted to Catterall Hall. Once the isolated residence of Arnwood falls is left behind, cross a hedge stile and watch for the start of the riverside trail.

Straddle the fence stile and accompany the meandering watercourse of the Wyre downstream to the foot suspension bridge near the hall.

Once over the river, amble along the raised embankment to the back gate of St Helen's churchyard.

It has been suggested that Celtic missionaries founded the original church on their way up the River Wyre in coracles. Henry IV provided huge timber beams in the roof.

It is certainly of venerable antiquity and the solid oak door remains unlocked for those who are seeking a brief spell of quiet reflection inside. This is encouraged by a quotation to be found in the south aisle – 'he who talks aloud in church talks only to the devil'.

Complementing this assertion, one could do worse than heed the thoughts of a local scribe before entering these hallowed portals:

'Enter this door
As if the floor
Within were gold
And every wall
Of jewels
All of wealth untold.
As if a choir
In robes of fire
Were singing here.
Nor shout, nor rush
But hush....
For God is here.'

The church lies at the head of the main street of Churchtown. Now by-passed, most travellers hurry westwards, bound invariably for Blackpool's acknowledged attractions and unaware that this most charming of villages even exists. And what a delightful sojourn they deny themselves. Quaintly reminiscent of a bygone age, picturesque cottages line the quiet street in front of the church.

Take the first right along the course of the old road to the Horns Inn where a friendly meeting was conducted that was to end in tragedy. It all began one Saturday night in 1853 when three pals were enjoying a convivial drink at the inn. John Wilding, more popularly known as 'Blackburn Jack', suggested that the festivities be continued at the Rose and Crown near Catterall and magnanimously offered to pay for the drinks if his friends agreed.

Once they were settled in the new surroundings, Wilding refused to meet his obligation and became quite belligerent when pressed by the others. Always the mediator, William Pendlebury said the promise would be forgotten if Wilding would give them some tobacco which he duly did. Clearly the worse for having supped too much liquor, Wilding

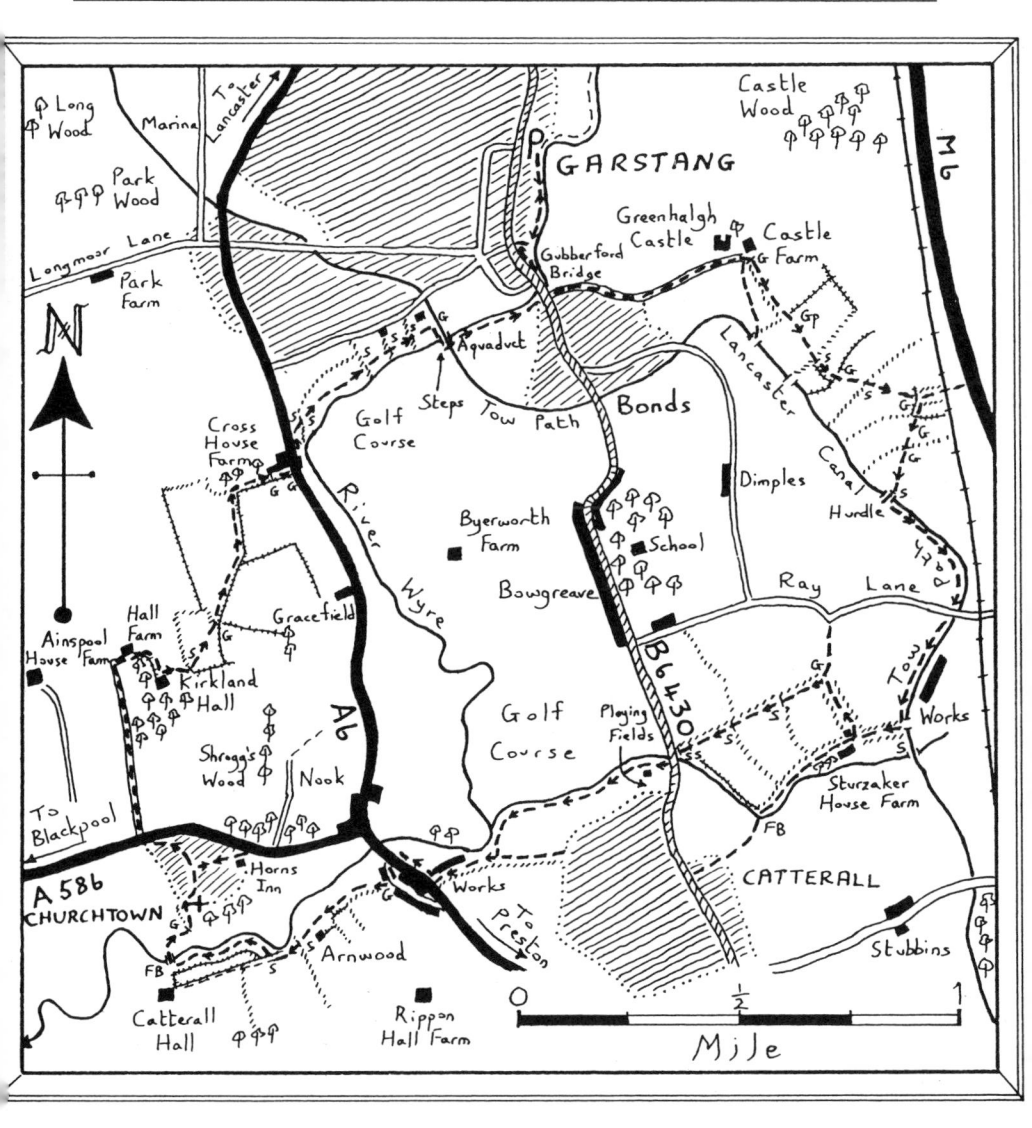

grew ever more obtuse and the trio parted soon after to avoid trouble. Some time later on the road to Garstang, a local tradesman met up with the inebriate who confessed to having 'stabbed one man twice, and another man once'. At the police station, the inebriated Wilding blurted out the whole sorry episode.

An officer despatched to locate the victims found Pendlebury lying in a pool of blood, clearly having taken his last drink. But of Thomas Rogerson there was no sign. It transpired that he had returned to his lodgings at Catterall to have his wound tended.

At his trial, Blackburn Jack was found guilty of manslaughter and sentenced to be transported to Australia for twenty years. An obvious lesson to other young men that excessive drink can easily transform a normally reticent individual into a bestial fiend. Wilding may not have intended to terminate his friend's life but that is no excuse for such depraved lunacy. He rightly paid a terrible price for his folly.

Retrace your steps along the old road, bearing right at the T-junction to the bypass. Another 50 metres on the far side is the access lane serving Hall Farm. At the end, lean right past the farmhouse to circle behind Kirkland Hall on a clear track. Secreted within a guard of trees, this once-substantial mansion has clearly experienced better days.

At the end of the track, cross a stile and take a diagonal course to the far side of the field, where a major track is joined. Pass through a gate and follow this (it is fenced on one side only) to Hagg Wood, turning right through the gated yard of Cross House Farm. Now on the busy A6 Garstang bypass, head left for 50 metres only. Cross with care to climb a stile in the opposite hedge. Drop down to another then fork into the bank of the River Wyre. Three further hedged stiles will find you crossing the playing fields of a local school on the edge of Garstang. A gate then gives access to the canal towpath.

Make a right over John Rennie's impressive aqueduct built in 1797. Descend the flight of steps on the far side to pass under the canal bridge and accompany the river along a clear path. At its terminus, the right of way goes under an archway that provides vehicular access to a nursing home. After emerging on the B6430 opposite Castle Lane, head left and retrace your steps back to the car park.

Fact and fantasy mingle effortlessly to cook up a fascinating blend of folklore in this part of the lovely Wyre Valley. So enjoy this melting pot of contrasting yet complementary ingredients.

Walk 13. Stocks-in-Bowland

The Drowned Village

Mysteries: Hark to Bounty GR 711524;
Stocks-in-Bowland GR 733558

Distance: 7 miles

Total Height Climbed: 600 feet (183 metres)

Nearest Shops: Slaidburn

Start and Finish: A large free car park is provided on the eastern
edge of Slaidburn, near to the River Hodder.

Map: Ordnance Survey 1:25 000 Outdoor Leisure 41, Forest of
Bowland & Ribblesdale

Slaidburn has changed little over the centuries and the rain-washed
stone cottages are an enduring and solid reminder of its ancient heritage. Any concession to modern living blends unobtrusively into the
rustic framework of this most captivating settlement. Only on the edge
do we detect the intrusion of that most potent symbol of contemporary
England – the car park, complete with toilet block. A necessary evil, it
thankfully does not detract from the period ambience that is preserved
intact. On a sunny day, most visitors are content to recline on the grassy
sward adjoining the river.

A glance at the map indicates that Slaidburn is a route focus where
four roads converge. In consequence, it became an important meeting
point and judicial centre for the whole of Central Lancashire. Even Oliver Cromwell is said to have held court on the top floor of what is now
the village inn. There was a separate access by means of an outside
stairway and the building assumed the role of the official courthouse after the original was demolished. Numerous artefacts are laid out as a reminder of the legal process in days gone by. No doubt the justice in
charge was assisted in his deliberations by frequent samplings of the
pub's liquid inventory. Could this be the derivation of the summons of
being 'called to the bar'?

Once known as The Dog, the current name stemmed from a hunt that

St James's was rebuilt above the flooded village of Stocks-in-Bowland

paused in front on the hostelry. When one of the hounds vented its impatience at the delay to the proceedings in the usual manner of such creatures, the master was heard to utter those immortal words, 'Hark to Bounty'. The name stuck and the inn is now one of the most celebrated in the county. A second pub called the Black Bull has long since ceased to be a purveyor of potent beverages and is now a youth hostel.

The Walk

Following a stroll up the main street of Slaidburn, head north along the lane that soon crosses Croasdale Beck. On the far side of the bridge, pass through a kissing gate and aim for a wall corner ahead. Follow the wall over a stile and along to cross the River Hodder by Holmehead Bridge. Then accompany the farm track to Hammerton Hall. One of the most influential families in the district during the Tudor era, members of the family were much given to riotous conduct that on one occasion led to murder.

Beyond a gate, circle right towards another gate then go straight up the rising bank with a wall on your right. After the next gate, the track soon enters a confined fence/wall corridor with a wedge of conifers on the left. The lower reaches of Stocks Reservoir can now be seen in the shallow depression to the left.

At the end of the corridor, mount a stile to continue ahead over Ten Acre Hill to a gate sited on the right of a small copse. Follow the edge of the trees down to Black House. Through the gate, take a left along the farm access track all the way to the reservoir road beyond Rushton Hill. The highest point offers an open vista across the elongated reach of Stocks Reservoir, flanked by the verdant blanket of Gisburn Forest.

Located to the right of the island in the middle lie the drowned remnants of the village known as Stocks-in-Bowland. Not as renowned as its Lake District counterpart of Mardale Green, it was an equally traumatic ordeal for the villagers to witness the creeping waters slowly devouring their homes. Where once the familiar sounds of village life filtered across the tranquillity of Stocks, the strident call of nesting birds now prevails. Twitchers and ramblers are a more common sight these days than the shepherd of old. It was 1926 when the water authorities opened the tap that effectively ended centuries of human endeavour at Dalehead in order to supply the burgeoning population of the Fylde.

The only building to survive was St James's which was rebuilt with stone from the original church at the sharp bend in the fell road where the track from Black House terminates. One of the most resolute clerics to preach at Dalehead was the Reverend Castle. Like his name, the vicar exuded strength and toughness as befits an ardent outdoorsman. But to the consternation of locals, he also denounced the widespread pursuit of salmon poaching.

In order to persuade the good reverend that this activity was normal practice amongst dales folk, a prime specimen was nailed to the vicarage door with the sound advice scrawled on a note that he should, 'Tak it and say nowt.'

With this bold thought in mind, continue heading due east up the road past the church, which soon enters the forest proper. After 200 metres and at a bend in the road, take a signposted path on the right that meanders through the trees to a walled stile at the far side. Then head half left across an open field to a gate at the far side. A short track with two more gates takes you past Lower Barn on a clear track that terminates at the access track serving Brook House Green. Make a slight detour left to gain the far side of the stream.

Boasting a name like Dugdale makes me feel at home in this part of the county. Even the watercourses have appropriated this aristocratic designation. Mount a stepped wall stile and stride out across the rough, open moorland, keeping left of a rising knoll. Aim for the distant building on the horizon. Your way is pathless and marshy in places but locate a stile 50 metres left of a wall corner and a small hut. Cross the next field to pass through a fence gap and up the facing slope. Keep left of a fence to reach a gate on the left of Higher Stony Bank.

Now take a right along the B6478 for half a mile, turning right down the access track serving Standridge. Pass through the farmyard, bearing left at the main house up to a gate. Slant right across to a hedge, which should be followed over the crest of a broad hill. Beyond a fence gap, keep right of the circular arbour known as Pikefield Plantation. Clearly grown for a purpose – any ideas?

All around, the undulating foothills encircling the Bowland Fell country form a green scarf that provides interesting terrain for walkers. Few people venture off the main tracks so you will be certain of a tranquillity that is precious and something to be preserved. Aim for the mid-point of a wall ahead to mount a stile then follow the fence down towards Higher High Field, forking right to climb a fence stile after 200 metres. Our route passes right of the farm buildings to join a wall corner across the field. Halfway along, mount a stepped stile and continue on the far side down to another. Next cross a footbridge over a narrow, tree-lined brook.

Over the track serving Lower High Field, slant half right to a wall stile. Lean away from the fence/wall on the left to reach the far side of the field and an indistinct ladder stile. Now stroll down to a gate near the field corner, accompanying the wall on your left to its termination at a stiled fence. Beyond this, aim for the left corner and a fence stile followed almost immediately by another to descend a steepening bank down to the farm below. Keep right of this and a gate will deposit you back on the B6478. Make a right over the languid flow of the Hodder back to the Slaidburn car park.

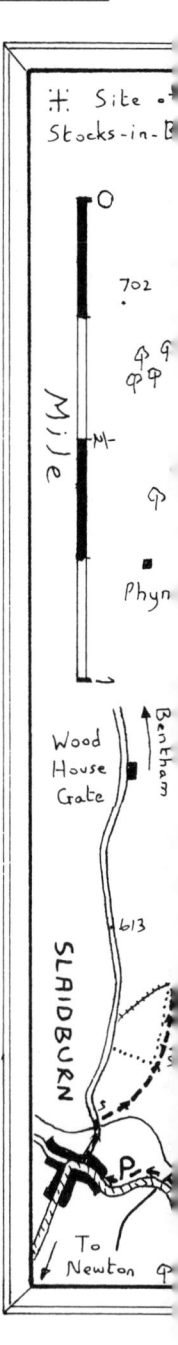

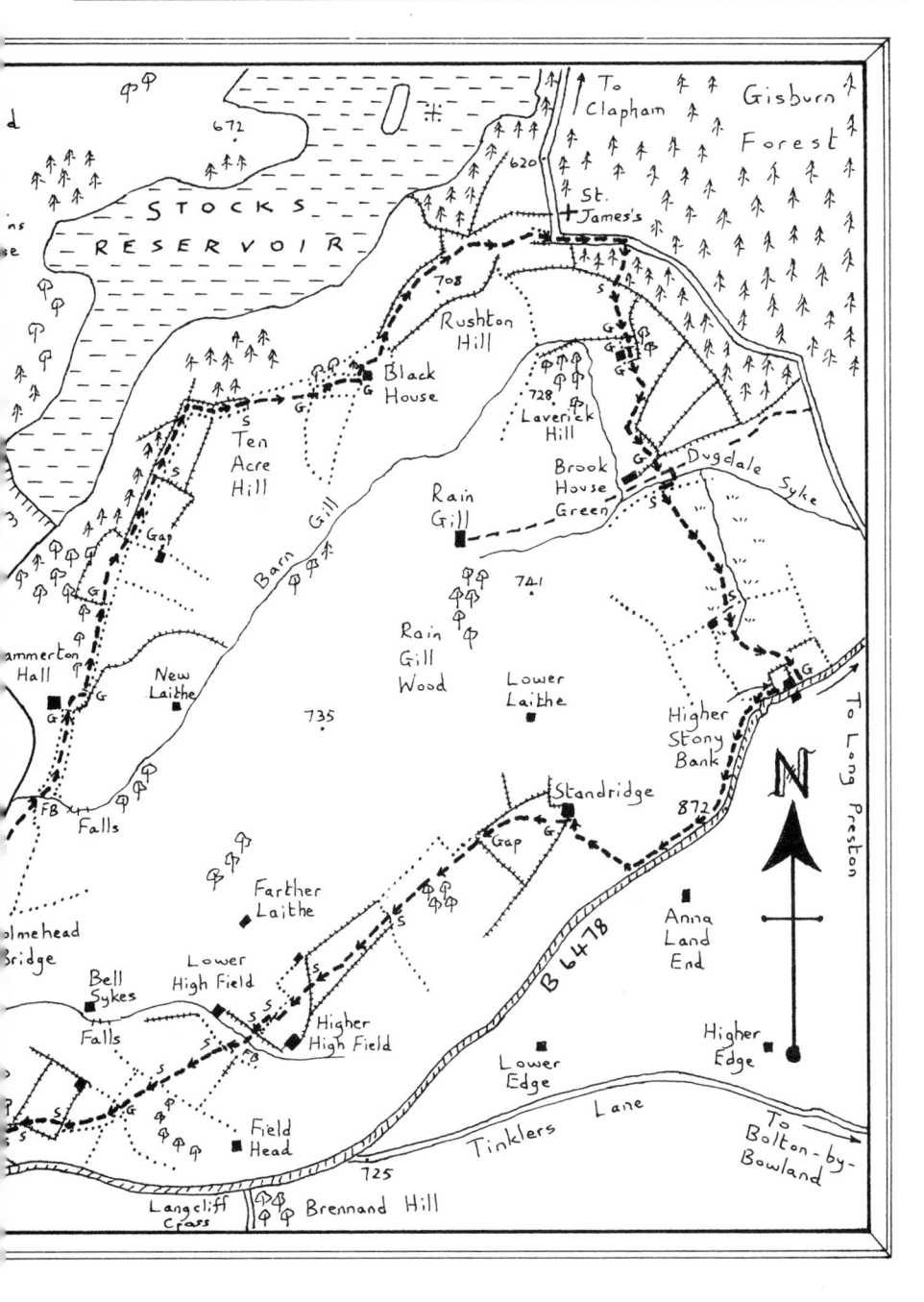

Walk 14. Kirkham

Here Yesterday, Gone Today!

Mystery: Mowbreck Hall GR 428333

Distance: 5½ miles

Total Height Climbed: Nil

Nearest Shops: Wesham

Start and Finish: Park close to Wesham Hall on the appropriately named Park Lane, off Mowbreck Lane in Wesham GR 422333.

Map: Ordnance Survey 1:25 000 Pathfinder 679, Preston (North) and Kirkham

When is a haunted house not a haunted house? Answer: When it's a caravan park. Burnt to the ground in recent years, absolutely no trace of Mowbreck Hall remains for the dedicated paranormal investigator to examine. Even the resident ghost appears to have been despatched to a retirement home on cloud nine. Today, we can but strain our imaginations to their limits in order to conjure up visions of the abhorrent denizen that once roamed the hall's gloomy corridors.

Once the seat of a renowned Papist family who defied the newly declared edicts of the Church of England in the 16th century, Mowbreck Hall became a haven for maverick Catholics in the area. When ordered to desist from harbouring such seditious insurgents, John Westby steadfastly thumbed his nose at the establishment of the day. Continued defiance of ecclesiastical laws by the 'rebellious minded' Westbys led to harsh fines being imposed. Yet still Mowbreck Hall remained a haven for fractious priests. One of these was Father Vivian Haydock who became infamous with regard to the sinister legend that grew up around him.

On a certain Hallowe'en, the good father (in both senses of the word owing to his having been a late entrant to the priesthood) was about to take midnight mass in the chapel attached to the hall. Being unaware that his son had been arrested for papist insurrection and executed, he was not prepared for the shock that awaited him on the tolling of the midnight hour. The blood-spattered head of George Haydock rose slowly above the altar and croaked out the Latin epithet, 'Tristitia Vestra Vertetur in Gaudium.' This translates as 'Your sadness is turned to joy'. What did he mean?

Father Haydock was given no opportunity to speculate as he collapsed from shock on perceiving the gory apparition. He never recovered and died soon after, his body being laid to rest at Cottam Hall – GR 504322. Numerous sightings of the gruesome appendage have been reported and many locals would not venture into the grounds of Mowbreck Hall after dark. Now that a village of mobile homes has taken root here, I have often wondered if the ghost of George Haydock has teamed up with another local celebrity who was driven from her home. The legendary Witch of Wesham, Meg Shelton, lived at Cuckoo Cottage hereabouts until she moved to Catforth. But that is a story we will investigate further in Walk 15.

Mowbreck Hall has gone, but Wesham still remains.

The Walk

This walk begins opposite the entrance to Mowbreck Caravan Park, GR 426335. Cross a stile and go through a thin scarf of trees, then over another stile to enter a large field. Slant half left across to the far side, taking note that the Fylde is a rich farming area and some of the fields might well have been planted with crops. Go over a stile and cross half right over a very large field, aiming right of a tree-fringed pond.

Beyond the pond, locate a stile in the kink of the fence in front. Then follow the edge for 50 metres before striking across the field, passing Carrot Wood on the left and so to a ladder stile. Make a beeline for the fence corner ahead then stroll along this to the edge of the westbound carriageway of the M55.

Cross the stile and head west towards a flight of steps that will bring you to the farm bridge serving Pasture Barn. Cross the motorway and go down a short, fenced corridor to climb a stile. Bear half left across the field to the edge of Medlar Wood. Mount a rickety stile and head right along the field boundary if crops are growing. At the corner, head left to locate a stile halfway along the hedge. This is crossed and a northerly direction maintained on the far side. At the next field corner bear right to the field edge where another stile is mounted. Accompany the hedge on your right to the farm access road adjacent to South Greenhills.

Continue along the rough road to North Greenhills, taking note that hills in this area are a distinct rarity. Prior to reaching this farm, slant left over a low fence to head west alongside a hedge. Watch for a concealed stile in the hedge after 100 metres. After crossing this, chaperone a fenced stream, once again heading north, and go over one stile before arriving at a footbridge. After crossing the narrow brook, follow the fence on your left over a stile to a major field service track. Hedged, but only partially on the right side, keep with this until it merges with a back lane adjacent to Medlar Hall.

Continue down to Leyland Hall, where the lane is abandoned in favour of a track that maintains a southerly course. It bends right of Solarium Nurseries, over a tubular metal stile, and then alongside a hedge. On the occasion I come this way, the glasshouses were being used to nurture conifers, a tree normally associated with cold climates.

Once the next stile has been negotiated, pass a large pond on the left and stroll to the eastbound carriageway of the motorway. Bear right for 200 metres to cross Medlar Brook by a stile and so to another before mounting a flight of steps to gain the motorway junction.

Circle the roundabout, slanting left along the A585 for Kirkham. After 100 metres and opposite a side road, head left at Old Cottage. A stile gives onto a field that is soon crossed, along with the continuing Medlar Brook via a footbridge. Bear left around the edge of the field to its far corner. There head right down the opposite side and follow a hedge to reach the access road serving Pasture Barn.

Pass the tiny Moat Wood on the left then a left wheel through a gate brings you back into the fields. Accompany the hedge now on your right to a stile at the far end. Continue in a straight line across the next four fields, the right of way avoiding marshy ground to the right. After four

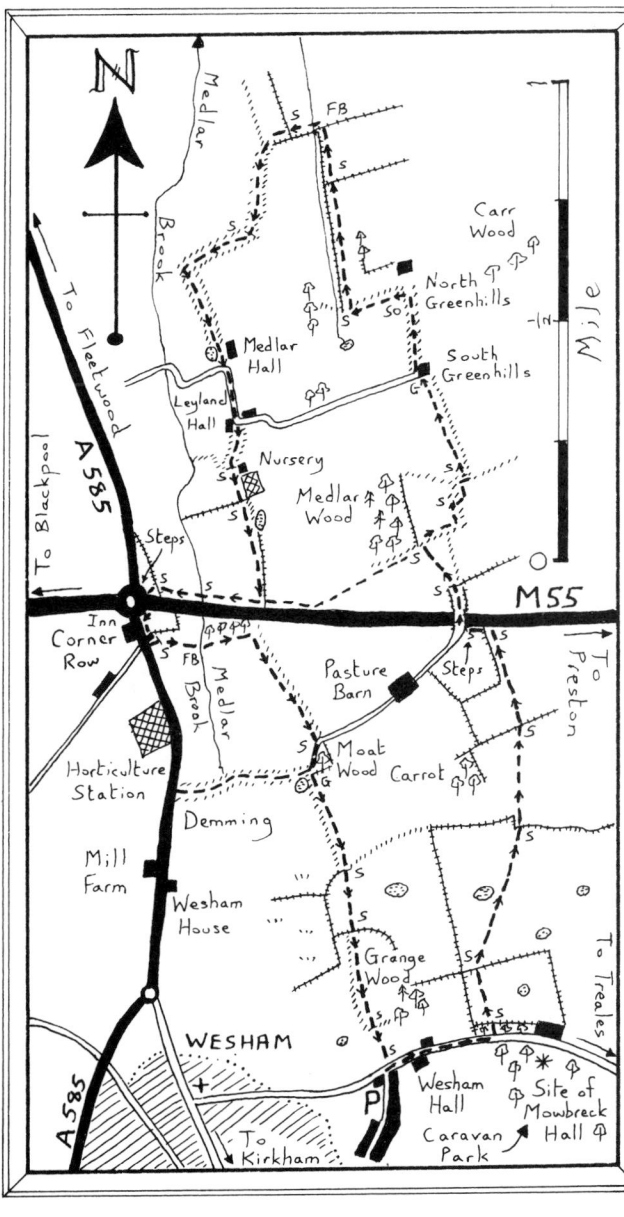

stiles you should find yourself back in Mowbreck Lane, almost opposite our starting point.

Typical countryside associated with the Fylde (the flat terrain of underlying sandstone) provides easy walking with no ascents of any kind, unless you count the two flights of steps. It may not be the most nerve-shattering walk of those on offer, owing to the demise of Mowbreck Hall, but is nonetheless a joy to follow.

Walk 15. Woodplumpton

Witch is the Right Grave?

Mystery: The Fylde Witch GR 499344

Distance: 5 miles

Total Height Climbed: Nil

Nearest Shops: Woodplumpton

Start and Finish: Parking is available adjacent to St Anne's graveyard in Woodplumpton.

Map: Ordnance Survey 1:25 000 Pathfinder 679, Preston (North) and Kirkham

Originally situated close by a plum tree on the edge of the extensive forest that stretched away towards the Bowland Fells, Woodplumpton has a much more ancient pedigree than a cursory glance might suggest. As one drives down the main street, there is little to interest the casual visitor until the church of St Anne is reached. Approached through an august lych gate, with the old stocks close by, Christian worship has been conducted here since the 11th century. The present structure was built in 1639. The unusual bell cote further augments the church's architectural appeal. But what really marks St Anne's apart from its neighbours can be found at the side of the path near the main entrance.

Look closely and you will certainly spot a prodigious boulder under which lie the remains of Marjorie Hilton, better remembered hereabouts as the Fylde Witch. More commonly referred to as Meg Shelton, any underhanded, conniving mischief that occurred in the district was laid at Meg's door (more specifically Cuckoo Cottage at Wesham). Perhaps she was a cantankerous old crone, maybe also prone to fits of bad temper. 'Crafty, deceitful, sly' and 'grasping' are just a clutch of epithets heaped upon the poor woman, but she was never actually caught in the act of turning the milk sour or encouraging stillborn calves.

One farmer who suspected her of stealing corn lay in wait on numerous occasions but was never able to catch her. One night he did see her enter the mill and on counting his sacks found there was one too many.

Lychgate and stocks outside St Ann's church, Woodplumpton

Seizing a pitchfork, he thrust it deep into each sack until a frightful yowl of pain rent the air. Meg leapt from the sack, jumped on her broomstick and never stole corn again.

A mythical tale to while away a wet afternoon in the Wheatsheaf Inn at Woodplumpton? Possibly. But Meg Shelton was certainly no figment of an over-imaginative populace. She did live at Wesham but spent most of her life in Catforth, where she is said to have arrived in bizarre circumstances. Meg struck a bewitching bargain with her landlord that involved her changing into a hare. If she succeeded in evading a chase by his dogs, the Catforth cottage would be hers. But the scheming landlord released an unduly rapid hound that snapped at her 'harey' heels, resulting in the distraught harridan sporting a limp thereafter. In the event, Meg did acquire the cottage and remained there until her death in 1705.

Crushed, it is said, betwixt a barrel and a wall, Meg Shelton was nonetheless adjudged to be worthy of a Christian burial as she had never been 'examined as a witch'. In essence, this involved a dubious meeting with the infamous ducking stool specially reserved for those accused of dabbling in the black arts. However, the good citizens of Woodplumpton determined that the ceremony should be in keeping

with the witch's lifestyle by burying her at dead of night. Not one to suc-
cumb gracefully, Meg caused more skulduggery in death than when
alive – to such an extent that a Cottam priest was called to perform an
exorcism.

And this time she was buried head down in a hole covered by the ti-
tanic rock that even today bears witness to Meg 's antics. This ruse appears to have been only partially successful in keeping the Fylde Witch
incarcerated. Rumours abound of sightings in the vicinity of the
church. One young boy entering ahead of his parents suddenly burst
through the doors in terror, claiming that a haggard old woman had
chased him out.

With such an active past, the spirit of Meg Shelton still appears to ex-
ert a mesmeric influence over the present congregation. On the day I
visited the grave a bunch of flowers had been laid against the
rough-hewn stone to the memory of Marjorie Hilton.

The Walk

At the end of the walkway, bear right between rows of neatly tended
plots to pass through a wall gap. Slant left to accompany a hedge to the
Whinneyfield Farm access lane. Bear left across the field to the corner
of a hedge and thence along to a gap on the left. After passing a large
pond, fork half right past a small coppice into the shallow depression
occupied by Woodplumpton Brook. Cross the footbridge and turn immediately right through a gate into a large, open field. Aim left of a pair
of trees to locate a gap in the hedge to the right of a reedy pond. Cross the
next field, slanting right alongside another hedge.

At the end of this field an untidy gap in dire need of a new stile gives
access to the adjacent field, followed immediately by a short footbridge
and stile. Continue west alongside the hedged stream to the next stile,
which is just beyond a field track from Swillbrook House. Initially
keeping with the stream, strike half right across the field and rejoin the
hedge that closes with Crown Lane next to the Free Methodist Church.

Take a left along Rosemary Lane, continuing ahead on a rough track
when the metalled road swings left. Keep left of the farm ahead, keeping
with an enclosed path that widens out after a gate. With a hedge on your
right only, walk along the grass track for 300 metres until a stile in the
hedge is reached.

Cross the field to a corner and then follow another hedge to gain a
back lane. Head right up this road. Once the canal bridge is crossed

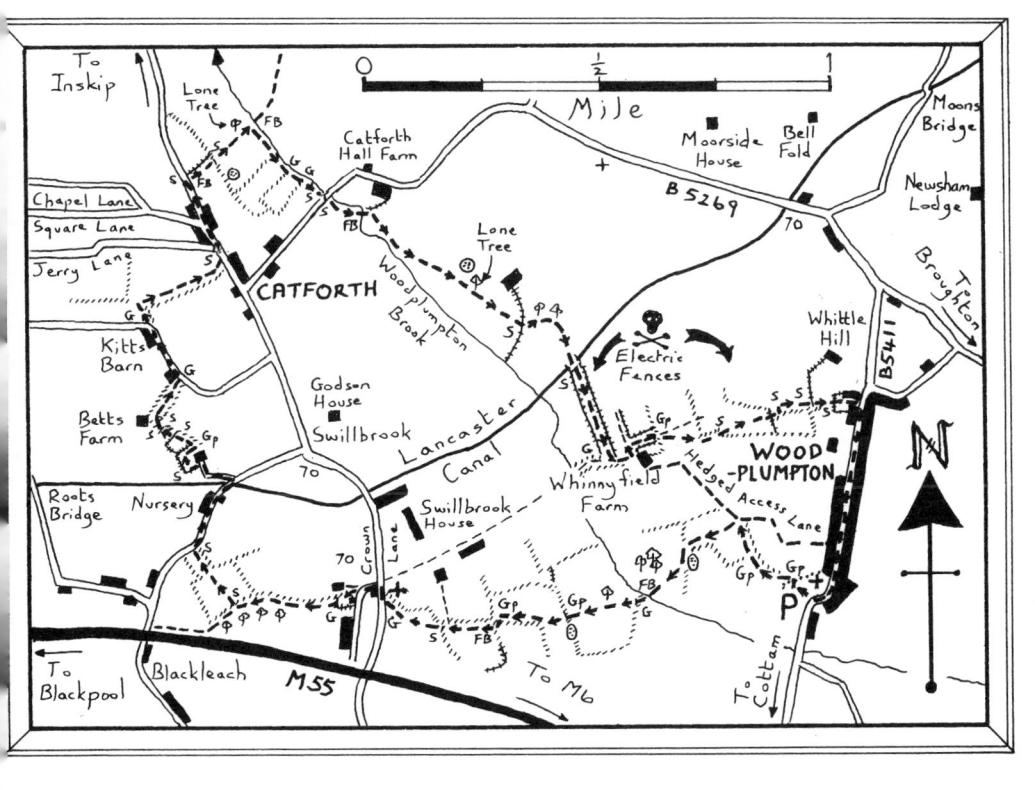

swing immediately left. Stroll up this access road to an isolated house, passing through a hedge gap on the left. Circle around the fenced boundary to the far side and over a stile to continue alongside a hedge to its limit.

Watch for a hidden stile sandwiched between hedge and fence before crossing a field corner and another stile onto the access track for Betts Farm. Walk up to bear left along a lane as far as Kitts Barn on the corner. Go straight over to pass through an old iron pedestrian gate and along to a corner. Bear right here then amble along the hedge to the main street of Catforth.

A series of parallel lanes links this thoroughfare with outlying farms, testifying to the agrarian influence on the village. At one time it was exceedingly marshy in these parts and much infilling and drainage was undertaken before permanent settlement could be established.

The Methodist sect has always enjoyed a strong following in the Catforth locality. Led by preachers known as 'ranters' on account of their fervent moralising, the faithful met in private houses prior to the building of their first church in 1829. Nothing has changed in Catforth in this respect, the modern building in Crown Lane ample testament to the Methodist grip in this part of the Fylde.

After passing Square Lane, watch for a stile and contiguous footbridge 100 metres north on the right. Accompany a fence for another 100 metres to a dual stile in a somewhat overgrown hedge. Cross the next open field past a lone tree, aiming for a footbridge spanning the deep cutting of Woodplumpton Brook. Bear right to follow the edge of the watercourse to the lane and Catforth Hall Bridge.

On the far side, continue onward to cross the brook by a footbridge then head south-east, taking a middle course across the elongated open field towards a solitary tree just past the large pond on the left. A fence stile is crossed soon after and a clear field track joined. Take a left circling round to cross the Lancaster Canal, after which a proliferation of electrified fencing demands care if shock tactics are to be avoided.

Head left at the end to take you through a gate and so to Whinneyfield Farm. Bear right then left along fenced tracks to clear the farm buildings. After passing through a gap in the hedge, lean half right towards a hedged corner and walk along to a concealed plank footbridge and stile giving onto the adjacent field. Then make a diagonal right-hand crossing of the field, aiming to the right. After the next stile, stroll along the right edge of the field. Two more stiles will bring you to an enclosed passage that emerges on a rough cul-de-sac at the edge of Woodplumpton. Slant right down the main street and back to St Anne's Church.

The image of Meg Shelton zipping about on her trusty besom is more likely to become apparent after leaving The Wheatsheaf somewhat later in the day. But even the most incredulous sceptic cannot deny her beguiling association with the area. The point where fact and fantasy merge has to be a matter of personal interpretation. So where do you draw the line?

Walk 16. Fernyhalgh

And All's Well at Chingle!

Mysteries: Ladyewell GR 556336; Chingle Hall GR 557358

Distance: 6 miles

Total Height Climbed: 150 feet (46 metres)

Nearest Shops: Goosnargh

Start and Finish: At the northern limit of Fulwood, immediately to the north of the M55 intersection with the A6, take the B6241 towards Broughton Hall. Bear left at the second roundabout to cross the M6 then take the first right to reach the dispersed hamlet of Fernyhalgh. Ample parking space is available along the lane between the nursery school and St Mary's Church.

Map: Ordnance Survey 1:25 000 Pathfinder 679, Preston (North) and Kirkham

---

Within sight and sound of the busy M6 motorway, Fernyhalgh presents the laid-back, easy-going appearance of a much more remote settlement. One could never imagine that this tranquil enclave lies only just outside the boundaries of the Preston metropolis. The name means 'ancient shrine' and offers a tantalising clue to Fernyhalgh's celebrity status.

Even way back in the Dark Ages a sacred well is known to have existed here. After walking down the road adjoining the church and old schoolhouse, take the first right, which leads round to Ladyewell. The shrine is located in a secluded grotto within the well-tended gardens of this Catholic retreat. Generations of pilgrims have come from many parts of England and beyond to imbibe the holy waters that are available to all visitors. If the inclination takes you, seek out the resident incumbent, Father Benedict Russillo, who is more than willing to provide a history of the shrine. Sit awhile and allow the calming ambience to wash over you. Nothing else is more likely to set worldly cares in their true perspective than a few minutes' quiet reflection by the well.

Legend suggests that an Irish trader shipwrecked off the Lancashire

The mythical spring at Fernyhalgh

coast beheld a vision after giving thanks for his safe deliverance from the storm. He was directed to a place called Fernyhalgh where he would find a crab-apple tree bearing fruit without cores and nurtured by a clear spring. Unsuccessful in his endeavour to locate the spring and about to give up the search, the merchant overheard a maid at his lodgings talking of the place. She duly led him to the spring where he erected a chapel dedicated to the Blessed Virgin Mary.

Over the centuries since that momentous event, many have testified to the healing powers of the well to the extent that it has become a noted shrine for the faithful and should be respected as such. Even during times of hardship when Catholics suffered great persecution, Ladyewell survived and prospered.

This old rhyme might well have been penned with walkers in mind:
'So – in peaceful merry dwell,
This tranquil spot, this ancient well,
And may Our Lady's blessing be
Rambling loiterer, e'er with thee.'

The Walk

After due deliberation at this special sanctuary, continue down the tree-girt path by the side of Ladyewell. Leaning at ungainly angles, it is little wonder that the telephone lines to the house have frequently been brought down. Perhaps the spirit of the Irish merchant is attempting to maintain the shrine's isolation. No bad thing in these times of mass communication, wouldn't you say?

At the end of the path, join the road serving Haighton House. A brief scan of the OS map intimates that this could provide a splendid walk through the wooded glen. And so it would but for the metalled access road. So instead, lean right over Fernyhalgh Bridge, which spans Savick Brook, and take the field track on the left just before the motorway bridge. At the top of a brief rise, fork right along a fence to a hedge at the far side of a pond. Thence continue along the right side of the hedge to a farm road. Bear left but do not enter the yard of Clock House Farm. Take a left along a broad, hedged track that bends left after 200 metres down a constricted channel into the valley of Savick Brook.

Head right at the bottom to accompany the wooded glen over two stiles to the access road for Haighton House. Slant left over Londonderry Bridge, taking the fenced path on the right that circles behind the cottage and kennels of the same name. Climb out of the vale along a stony track to a builder's yard. The path veers left round the outer edge to emerge on a paved service road. Head north-west past Dingle Wood on the right and a ruined farmhouse on the left.

Watch for the start of the right of way 100 metres beyond a ruin to fork right alongside a hedge. Proceed for another 200 metres then cross a stile into the adjacent field. Take a middle course to the far end, where a footbridge provides a through point. Go over a short grassy sward to a gate and then along a farm track to bring you to the road though the village of Haighton Green.

Bear left around a double bend in the road until the start of a footpath on the right, opposite a junction, is reached. Make a half left crossing of the field, keeping left of a wooded pond, one of many scattered throughout this rolling terrain. Look for a stile that allows passage along a hedge down into the shallow vale of Blundel Brook.

Beyond the next stile, watch for one in the hedge on the left. This indicates a right wheel over to the footbridge spanning the brook. Thereafter head north up a gentle rise to the right corner of the field. There mount a stile. Follow the continuing hedge on your right to its far end where a tree house (March 1998) tempts agile scramblers to occupy it for a lunch stop.

Cross two stiles to gain the far side of a sylvan tributary stream. Accompany the fence, heading right to another which has been recently erected to split the long field, but lacks a stile. Step over and make a diagonal foray over to Whittingham Hall. Gaunt and forbidding, the drab remnants of Whittingham Hospital present a sad façade to the world. Natural flora attempts with some measure of success to reassert itself over this empty shell of a once thriving community.

Whittingham once boasted of being the largest psychiatric hospital in Europe but was closed down when the policy of 'Care in the Community' became fashionable. Today, the decaying site awaits redevelopment, which is desperately needed if the spectral images of past residents are to rest in peace.

Turn your back on the bones of this sinister cadaver to make your way in a westerly direction on the right of a fence. At the end of the field, cross a double stile and slant left along a short, fenced corridor to gain the opposite side of the continuing hedged border via a third stile. Beyond an intermittent line of trees, make for a gate that provides access to the grounds of Chingle Hall.

Erected in the 13th century by Adam de Singleton, this mysterious dwelling is reputed to be the most haunted house in Lancashire. And should a chilly ripple dance a merry jig down your spine, be sure that the troubled entity pervading the environs of Chingle has announced its baleful presence.

Surrounded by a moat, it is unclear whether its purpose was to prevent attacks by vociferous invaders, or an attempt to contain the psychic forces within. The inner framework of the house is constructed from Norwegian oak believed to have originated from a wrecked Viking ship discovered in the Ribble Valley. Bolt-holes, hides and escape routes abound, their aim to prevent the capture of priests during periods of Catholic persecution. When an illicit mass was in progress, a candle was placed in the small signal window located in the porch to summon the faithful to prayer. Could it be that harassed pilgrims were sent here when Ladyewell was under close scrutiny from the authorities?

Cloaked in secrecy, an air of mystery helps to promote the bizarre legend of the 'headless ghost'. This nebulous wraith is said to be John Wall who occupied the hall during the reign of Charles I. After becoming a Franciscan monk he was raised to sainthood in 1679, having suffered the ultimate fate of being hanged, drawn and quartered for his beliefs.

His head is thought to be concealed somewhere in the labyrinth of nooks and crannies that riddle Chingle Hall. Until documents relating to his death are discovered, the haunting will no doubt continue. Numerous sightings have been reported in recent times of a cowled figure

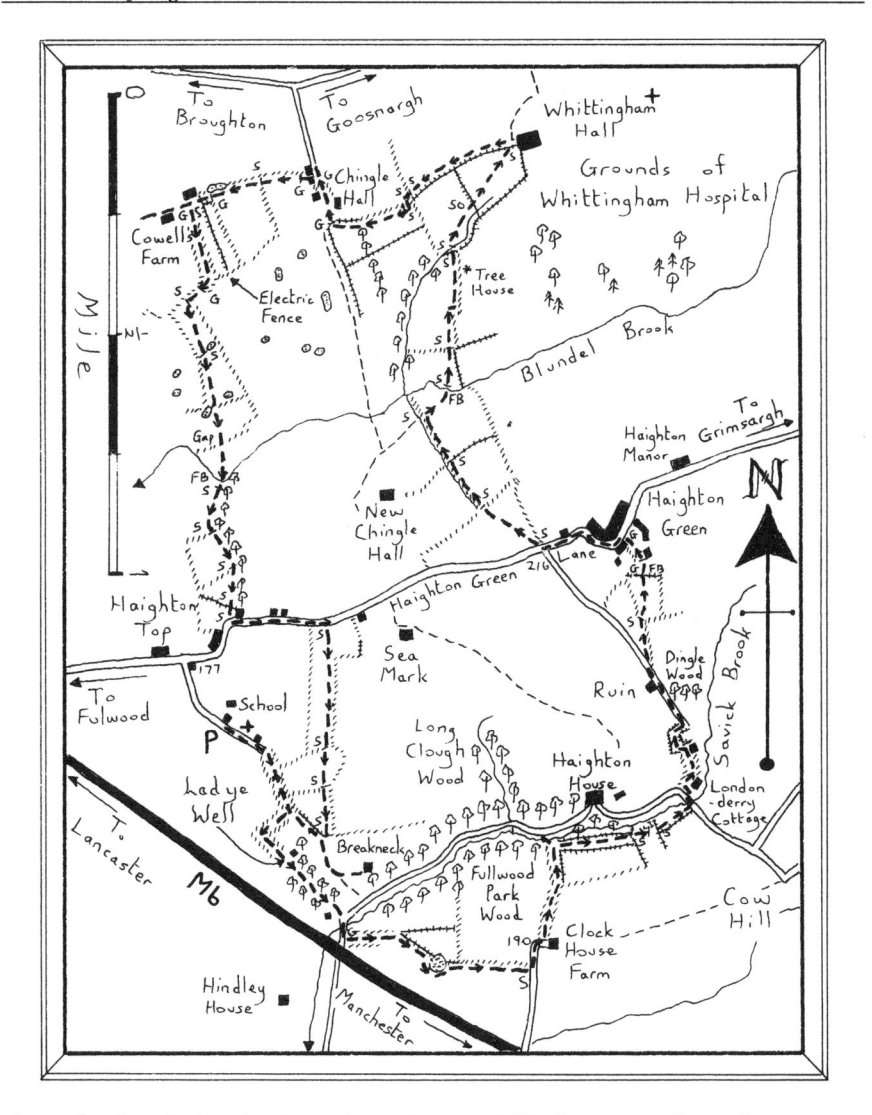

described as being 'pale and not human'. He has even been known to cause motorists in the vicinity to suddenly brake hard and has clearly not learned the Green Cross Code during his long residence at Chingle.

On one occasion, a stalwart upholder of the law ignored the measured tread of boots on the wooden upper floor. But when the sound of a body being dragged across the floor and a rattling of chains caused consternation amongst other dinner guests, a search of the hall was organised. Nothing was found. This is just one example of the unexplained phenomena that have attracted the attention of paranormal investigations and make Chingle Hall such a charismatic building.

After due regard for this unique structure continue down the lane towards Goosnargh, taking the second gate on the left between red-brick farm buildings. Pass through a gate at the far end and accompany a hedge in a west-south-west direction – first over a stile then past a large pond to a gate, after which there is another stile.

Circle left of the farmyard to locate a gate at the far side. Head left down a rough lane and into a field at the bottom. After crossing a flat bridge, lean right to mount a stile in the facing hedge. Follow the churned-up farm track around the edge of this field and past a tree-girt pond before bearing sharp left into the next field. Continue alongside a hedge on your right until the track peters out above yet another pond. Drop down an easy grass slope, aiming for a gap in the hedge at the bottom. Then cross over Blundel Brook on a solid footbridge. Follow a line of trees to the south over five stiles – this should bring you to Haighton Green Lane.

Bear left along the road for a quarter of a mile until a footpath stile on the rights points the way south. Join a hedge after 100 metres and accompany it to the end of this long, narrow field to cross a stile. Maintain a southerly course over dipping ground to another stile and then follow a hedge to join the access road serving Breakneck Farm.

Turn right for the return to Fernyhalgh and the termination of a walk enjoying a unifying mystique. The pious reflection of the Ladyewell shrine appears to contrast markedly with the haunting aura that pervades Chingle Hall yet the common bond of religious torment inextricably links both and it is to the spirit of self-sacrifice that this walk is dedicated.

Walk 17. Longridge

Milk Cow Blues

Mystery: Dun Cow Rib GR 596376

Distance: 6 miles

Total Height Climbed: Insignificant

Nearest Shops: Longridge

Start and Finish: Approach Longridge along the B5269 from the direction of Broughton then turn left up Halfpenny Lane and park in the lay-by immediately on the left, adjacent to a telephone kiosk.

Map: Ordnance Survey 1:25 000 Pathfinder 679, Preston (North) and Kirkham

---

From the lay-by, walk up Halfpenny Lane for a quarter of a mile until you reach a renovated stone farmhouse on the left. It originates from the early Stuart period according to the date above the main door. Cast your eye above the portico where a crescent-shaped object emblazons the coat-of-arms carved by the first inhabitants. Now grey and severely weathered with age, it is easily passed by unnoticed.

Taken from a robust dun-coloured cow, this relic has been passed down through generations, clearly indicating a history of some significance. The story is told of a time when prolonged drought sucked the last vestige of moisture from the land around Longridge, turning the grass brown and destroying crops. As most people in those days depended on farming for their livelihood, this was a desperate situation. Cattle grew thin and emaciated through lack of nourishment, as did the local populace in their turn. When all seemed lost and starvation stretched out its greedy tentacles, a large, healthy-looking cow was seen wandering alone on the edge of Longridge Fell.

After it was brought down to the farm in Halfpenny Lane and found to be unaffected by the drought, local people were allowed to come and fill their buckets with the life-giving fluid. The dun cow continued to supply their needs, undaunted by the dry conditions. But dark clouds were approaching, and not of the kind to be welcomed by rain-starved farmers. No, indeed. A malevolent witch who delighted in causing mayhem amongst her neighbours came to hear of the vital role being enacted by the dun cow. With a spiteful cackle, the old harridan came to the cow in her turn and proceeded to draw milk into a sieve.

The rich white nectar poured through and soaked into the parched earth as the cow continued to supply her beneficence, innocently unaware of the vindictive trickery being performed. Slowly, the poor beast became exhausted until finally, emptied of her boon, she collapsed and died. Hallowed throughout the area as a munificent saviour, one of the cow's ribs was taken and placed above the door of the farm that was ever after known as Old Rib as a lasting memorial. Although much gnarled and bent with age, here it still remains. A totem that would appear to have paid dividends to those who live here – so long as the rib remains in place, of course.

Once, it was removed and cast into Charnley Brook on the far side of Longridge by some foolhardy prankster. Until the rib was returned to its rightful place, the thoughtless poltroon was beset by all manner of dire misfortunes. But what became of the rascally broom-rider was never established. Could she have been the one who removed the sacred relic, only to have the tables turned against her? Those who cause mayhem shall be repaid in kind.

The Dun Cow Rib still hangs above the farmhouse door.

The Walk

Thinking on such an apt form of recompense, carry on up Halfpenny Lane past Old Rib Farm for 200 metres before crossing a stile on the left to accompany a hedge to another road. Bear left for another 200 metres, then swing right along Old Clay Lane, the entrance being marked by a ·pair of heavy iron gates usually left open.

A broad, hedged track, once an access route for clay pits used in the manufacture of pipes and tiles, it has become rather overgrown through disuse. Beyond a stile it opens out as far as the appropriately named Tile Croft, where a gate brings us to the access lane. Bear left along a clear track leading to Lancaster Farm.

Before reaching the farm, our way slants left along a fenced corridor with a gap at the end. Pass through this, followed soon after by another. Keep on the left side of the field boundary hedge. Negotiate a stile then veer half left across a confusing field, passing right of two small ponds. Maintain a north-westerly course to arrive at a gate and stile. At the end of the wide, hedged passage, avoid Withinreap Farm by heading left across a field where a footbridge is provided. There follows a short walk over to a bend in the road close to Holwood.

Go over the bend stile then immediately over another on the left and a plank footbridge. Assume a south-westerly direction alongside the fence on your left. Cross another footbridge at the far side and then walk over the next field parallel to the fence on the left. Once across this one, bear right along a track to pass through the first gate on the left to maintain the south-west course along a hedge.

Go through the gate ahead and circle half right towards the gate giving onto a back lane. Take a stroll right along here for half a mile. As Kidsnape is neared, watch for an unusual tree on the left with numerous sprouting talons – particularly evident in spring.

When the road bends sharply to the right, nip through a gate on the left along an overgrown corridor. Should you be clad in shorts, beware the rasping kiss from an abundance of stinging nettles. After 100 metres, a footbridge provides a dry crossing of Mill Brook. Lean right along the stream to a barrier fence, following it round to pass through the first gate into the adjoining field.

A path begins well as it slants half left across the field, but fades in mid-course. Stick with a south-south-east course, keeping left of a pond to pass through an intermittent line of trees. The far side is soon reached where another tributary of Mill Brook is negotiated via a disintegrating footbridge. Rotten with age, it is in much need of repair so take care.

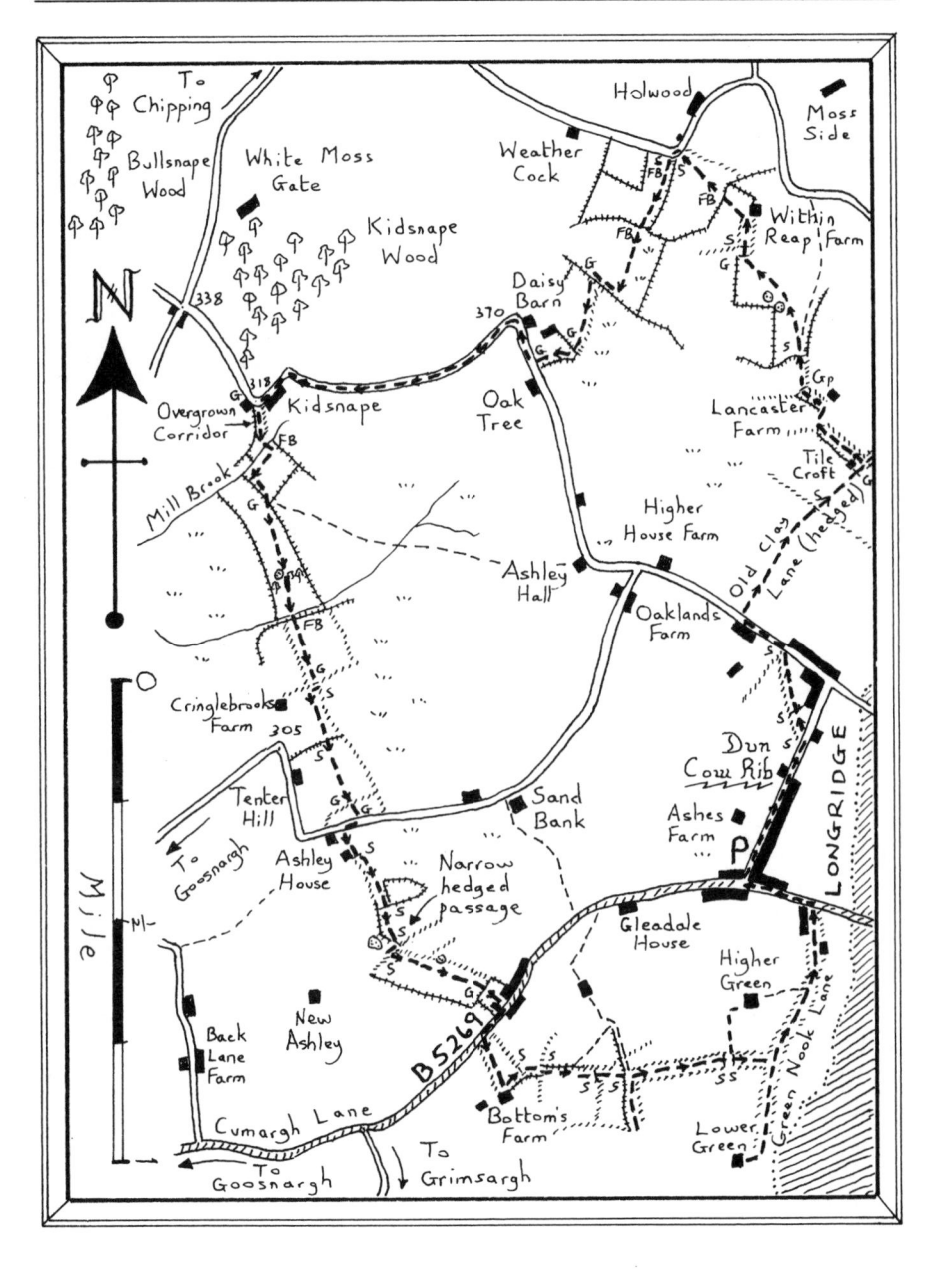

Accompany the hedge on the right to a corner where a stile gives access to the opposite field, after which the hedge is on the left. Mount the next stile to cross the middle of the field to a gate and another soon after which deposits you in a back lane close to Tenter Hill. this is something of a misnomer as hills in this locality are merely low blips in the gentle swell of the terrain.

Take a right then left down a paved farm road to climb a stile on the left into the adjacent field. Stroll down the hedge, funnelling into a fenced corridor with a stile at its terminus. Continue along the fence on the right to cross a stile at the far corner. A brief connecting passage of 50 metres enables the next onward field to be reached.

Keep with the hedge on your left down to a gated fence then go round to the right to join the B5269. Bear right for 100 metres before taking the track on the left to Bottom's Farm. Leave this before reaching the buildings to cross rough ground on the left aiming for a stile in the hedge. Another follows soon after as you now head due east with a fence on your left. Ignore a major track forking left to continue onward to reach the field end.

Maintain a straight course across the next field to link with a prominent hedged track. Stiled at either end, it merges with that serving Higher Green Nook. On reaching Green Nook Lane, head left back to the main road where another left will return you to Halfpenny Lane.

Walk 18. Chipping

Spooks Galore!

Mysteries: The Sun Inn GR 623433; Leagram Hall GR 625441

Distance: 5½ miles

Total Height Climbed: 350 feet (107 metres)

Nearest Shops: Chipping

Start and Finish: A free car park is available in the centre of Chipping.

Map: Ordnance Survey 1:25 000 Outdoor Leisure 41, Forest of Bowland & Ribblesdale

Conjure up any word or phrase that evokes images of the classic English village and all could be applied to Chipping. Even though it is remote from the major traffic arteries serving Lancashire and the North, the village has failed to hide itself away among the rolling foothills of South Bowland. Although a honey-pot for cyclists and walkers, its narrow streets remain unchanged from when the village was a hive of industry. Mills powered by the surging torrent of Chipping Brook brought prosperity through the forging of brass and woodcraft. Tucked away on the outside of Chipping, a modern factory still makes high-quality chairs and does nothing to detract from the rustic charm.

Numerous gift shops and public houses cater for the needs of a new industry that attracts people from all over Lancashire who value its past heritage. From the car park, take a stroll down past St Bartholomew's Church to the main square. The influx of motorised transport has no place on the narrow streets of Chipping and hold-ups are a frequent but inevitable result of 'progress' at busy times. In consequence, an out-of-season visit is recommended.

The ghost of a barmaid called Lizzie Dean who lived there in the 18th century reputedly haunts the Sun Inn. Engaged to a local man, she discovered the hard way that the rascally fiancé had made other plans behind her back. When she saw him escorting a new bride up the church path on the supposed day of her wedding, the shock was too much for poor Lizzie to comprehend. She was inconsolable and hanged herself in the pub where she worked.

But the girl was astute enough even in grief to leave written instructions that her body should be buried under the same church path. Her idea was to remind the callous rogue of his treachery each time he went to church. Perhaps only those with a guilty conscience will witness the chilling appearance of Lizzie Dean's ghost in the Sun Hotel, or feel the deathly presence in the churchyard. And they are unlikely to tell, are they?

Ye Olde Worlde main street of Chipping

The Walk

Amble off up the road heading north west towards Garstang then fork right down a side lane to the old mill village. The workers' cottages originally used as a workhouse for the poor until 1840 have now been abandoned and are badly in need of some renovation. Huge amounts of logs indicate that industry in this part of rural Lancashire at least is a thriving prospect.

Just beyond the old cottages and opposite the mill pond, cross a stile on the right and climb a steepening bank alongside a fence. At the top of the rise, cross a fence stile continuing ahead to a new electric fence provided with a gate.

Glance over to the cluster of trees on your right behind which is secreted New Leagram Hall. Commanding an impressive vista across the Loud Valley towards Longridge Fell, the old hall was finally demolished in 1963. After centuries of peace in the family chapel, the family's remains were unearthed and reinstated in St Mary's Roman Catholic graveyard in Chipping.

Locals claimed that this disturbance would 'upset 'em no end to be amongst ordinary folk'. Surely not a dig at the snobbish attitude of the landed gentry in those class-riddled times. From that time, the hall and the immediate vicinity of the Leagram estates were haunted by spirits angered at having been awakened.

On the roads in the area, cars have stopped without warning; the drivers forced to abandon them when they would not restart. Strange figures have jumped out in front of vehicles and then promptly disappeared. Unearthly sounds have sprung from a nebulous mist that swathed the valley in its foetid embrace. All such apparitions might well be explained away logically, but not so the experience of a resident at Leagram Hall who was walking along the road in the direction of the fells. Observing three strangers walking in the opposite direction, she noted that no sound came from their boots, which should have been crunching on the gravel road. Her agitated dog suddenly broke the uncanny silence. Bending to calm the animal, the trio had disappeared when next she looked up. Immediately, the distraught hound began to fight with an invisible assailant. Eventually conceding defeat, it rushed off with a grievous yelp. The men instantly reappeared and chased after the dog. Although this bizarre incident occurred only on that single occasion, the dog would never again venture along that section of road.

Now drop down towards the wooded fringe of Dobson's Brook and go over a fence stile to cross the stream by a footbridge. Keep parallel

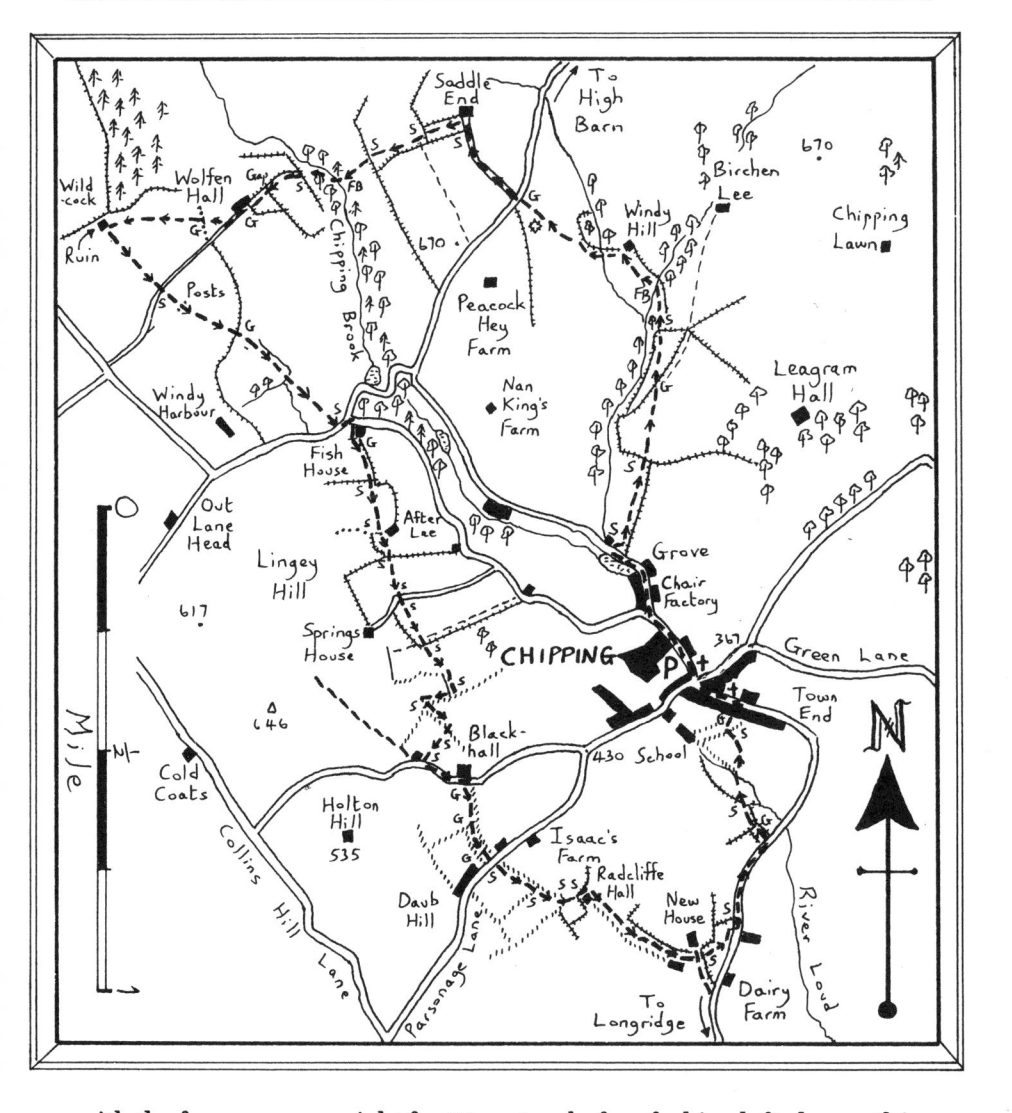

with the fence on your right for 50 metres before forking left along a thin track below Windy Hill Farm to merge with the access track. Accompany this to the road where the unusual circumstances of the phantom trio took place.

Cross straight over and take the access road to Saddle End. Just before the farm, cross a fence stile on the left and follow a thin path along the line of trees between two fences to another stile. Cross open pasture with a fence on your left to yet another stile linked to a gate. Lean half left down a gentle slope that steepens appreciably as you drop into the deep cutting of Chipping Brook. After crossing a footbridge, mount a stepped banking to reach a fence on the upper edge of the far bank. Beyond a stile, follow another fence along to Wolfen Hall, which is reached through a gate.

Named after a pack of wolves that roamed these lonely fells in the distant past, the hall was also well known as a refuge for thieves and brigands. No doubt it was regarded as a safe haven being remote from the nearest law enforcement agency.

Continue past the Hall for 50 metres and fork right off the access road. Once over a wall stile, slant right towards the accompanying fence, eventually reaching Wildcock House. This ruined farmstead lies at the foot of Parlick, the most southerly of the Bowland Fells. From here, head left along a dry gully to cross the Wolfen Hall road. After crossing the fence by a stile, pass between two isolated gateposts and maintain a south-easterly course down to a gate in a fence. Keep left after this to cross a small stream where another mingles from the right. Then continue down the field to meet Fish House Lane, heading left then right along the road signposted for Chipping.

Slip through the farmyard of Fish House on the right to emerge on a field track behind. Stick with the fence on your left over the first stile to cross a field, aiming to the right of a barn called After Lee. Pass through a narrow wall gap behind a row of trees and then over a patch of rough ground to mount a stile behind a kink in the fence. At the far side of the next field, cross straight over the access lane serving Strings House by two connecting stiles. Continue with a fence on the left. At the end of this field is a rough track where a fence stile is mounted.

At the far side of this next field it is necessary to deviate from the old line of the footpath by slanting left to the edge of the opposite field. Follow the boundary fence to a thick hedge and step over the stile in the field thus following its southern boundary for 100 metres until a stile is located. Over this, accompany another hedge for 50 metres only until a stile on the right is reached. Look for a wall gap at the far side of the adjoining field and make a beeline for it.

Emerge on a back lane next to an old cottage and head left down to Black Hall. Opposite there is a gate. Follow the hedge on your left to an enclosed passage gated at either end. Cross straight over the lane, ensuring that you climb the stile that enables you to continue on the right side of the field hedge. After negotiating two more stiles, cross a short grassy stretch to enter a cultivated arbour within the grounds of Radcliffe Hall.

A grass corridor brings you to the farmyard, where you should bear right down the access track. At the T-junction, cross over and go through a stile. Follow a sturdy fence and go over a small footbridge. Keep with a wire fence, aiming for the line of trees along the main road ahead. Step over this fence at a handy gap to parallel the road for 100 metres, until a stile deposits you on the Longridge road.

Take a left for 300 metres until an indented gate on the left points the way north back to Chipping across the fields. After following the fence on your right, climb a stile and then walk down a shallow bank to cross a minor stream by a stiled footbridge. Cross the large, open field, aiming for the mid-point of a hedge. Slant right after crossing a stile and walk through the school grounds to a gate on the left of the main building. A narrow passage exits on the main street, where a left will take you past John Brabin's Grammar School.

Now a private dwelling, it was founded by this entrepreneur from profits derived from the local textile industry. Pupils wore distinctive blue coats and could be instantly expelled if they failed to meet his exacting standards. Beyond the school, the street narrows appreciably and you soon arrive back in the square near the Sun Inn.

If you would like to learn more about Leagram Hall and the conservation work being undertaken by the estate owner, John Blundell-Weld, head right to edge of the village then left up a rising road for half a mile until you reach the entrance on the left. At present, only Friends of Leagram are allowed to view the re-created 19th century garden, but it is hoped to provide full public access in the near future.

The actress Penelope Keith, herself a keen gardener, is the first patron of the society which also conducts rural courses including photography, painting and archery. Diverse country walks that take in the variety of unusual flora are organised in what was formerly a royal deer forest. All that remains of the old hall is an arch that formed part of the Roman Catholic chapel where the family were interred until their resurrection and move to the Catholic cemetery.

Walk 19. Samlesbury

A Grave and Ghostly Undertaking

Mysteries: The Jealous Spouse GR 590304;
Samlesbury Hall GR 624305

Distance: 6½ miles

Total Height Climbed: 700 feet (213 metres)

Nearest Shops: Mellor Brook

Start and Finish: Parking is restricted along the A677 in the vicinity
of Samlesbury Hall. There is, however, a pull-in for two cars only at
the beginning of the walk – opposite the hall. No problems of this
nature will arise, of course, if you choose to investigate the hall
itself.

Maps: Ordnance Survey 1:25 000 Pathfinder 689 (Blackburn) and
680 (Longridge / Great Harwood); OS Explorer 19, West Pennine
Moors.

Prior to arriving at Samlesbury for the walk proper, call in at the church
of St Leonard-the-Less. Off the beaten track, the unusual name stems
from it being second-in-command to the mother church at
Walton-le-Dale. From junction 31 of the M6, head towards Blackburn,
turning left down Potter Lane after half a mile. The church is located on
the banks of the River Ribble, adjacent to a primary school. Its origins
stretch back into the faded mists of time. Inside is a feature known as
the 'invasion beam' which was used to bar the door to Celtic invaders
sweeping down from the north who were less than inclined to knock
before entering.

But our principal reason for seeking out this remote house of God is
to be found outside in the graveyard. A certain Tom Alker who attended
the church was married to a covetous lady whose intention was that he
should never be able to re-marry if she died first. And so it transpired.
Her threat to rise up from the grave and haunt the poor chap should he
err from the single status was soon put to the test following her demise.
Tom was, indeed, attracted to a local wench and was equally determined to curb his wife's virulent jealousy. Iron bars were riveted across

The hidden church of St Leonard-the-Less

the grave slab to prevent the spirit of the dead woman from leaving the plot to torment him.

The ruse appears to have succeeded: no reports of devilish intrigue having been reported thereafter by Tom Alker. Today the stone lies cracked and overgrown in the front section of the graveyard, the inscription worn away. This forgotten remnant from a hazy past can only be identified by means of the sawn-off bars. Since both Tom Alker and his wife are now communing on a higher plain, their removal is unlikely to encourage any further spiritual release.

The Walk

Say goodbye to the Alkers and St Leonard's, which is no less impressive in spite of its demeaning appendage, and continue on towards Samlesbury Hall which lies a further two miles up the Blackburn road. When gazing upon the half-timbered black and white splendour of the hall few people are aware that this is, in fact, the new hall. The original lies on the banks of the Ribble where it was savagely mauled by Scottish brigands in the 14th century.

In the middle years of the 16th century, John Southworth occupied the hall and is renowned for his zealous following of the Catholic faith – a dangerous undertaking after Henry VIII renounced the Church of Rome in furtherance of his matrimonial ambitions. After plotting to overthrow the newly established Church of England, Southworth was arrested and thrown into the Tower of London where he languished until his death in 1595. But his daughter is of much more interest to our investigations.

Dorothy Southworth fell in love with a De Houghton who just happened to be a Protestant. This was not a liaison that was likely to receive her father's blessing as you can imagine. Her brother, who overheard the pair planning to elope, hoped to safeguard the family from disgrace by ambushing the knight and his two companions. All three were killed in a bloodthirsty skirmish. Dorothy never recovered from her loss and spent the rest of her days in a convent, finally departing this mortal coil whispering her lover's name. In 1826, during excavations to construct the road by the hall, three skeletons were unearthed so adding credence to the story.

On numerous occasions over the years a lady in white has been seen floating around the corridors and grounds, moaning softly in search of her wasted lover. The ghost of Dorothy Southworth remains a potent entity in the folklore of Samlesbury Hall and certainly enhances the aura of mystery surrounding this noble estate.

Leave the vicinity of the hall by walking up Park Lane opposite and forking right up the access track which serves Hoolster Farm. Pass through the farmyard and over a ladder stile at the far side, forging ahead to join a hedge around the east side of Hoolster Hill. Beyond the next fence stile, continue onward to meet a back lane.

Head left for 400 metres, keeping an eye open for a concealed gap just past some cottages on the right. The right of way goes through the back garden and over the wall at the end. Accompany the wall on your left leaning away from the wall to go over the fence stile ahead.

Cross the field corner to another stile then aim for the far right corner of the next field to arrive at the access road serving Wallbanks House. Bear left along the road until it swings to the right. At this point, continue ahead down a constricted rough passage into the gloomy recess of Arley Brook. A claustrophobic silence enfolds this deep tributary cutting of the River Darwen, broken only by the gentle swish of the stream funnelling through the sylvan grotto.

After crossing a stone footbridge high above the valley floor, climb

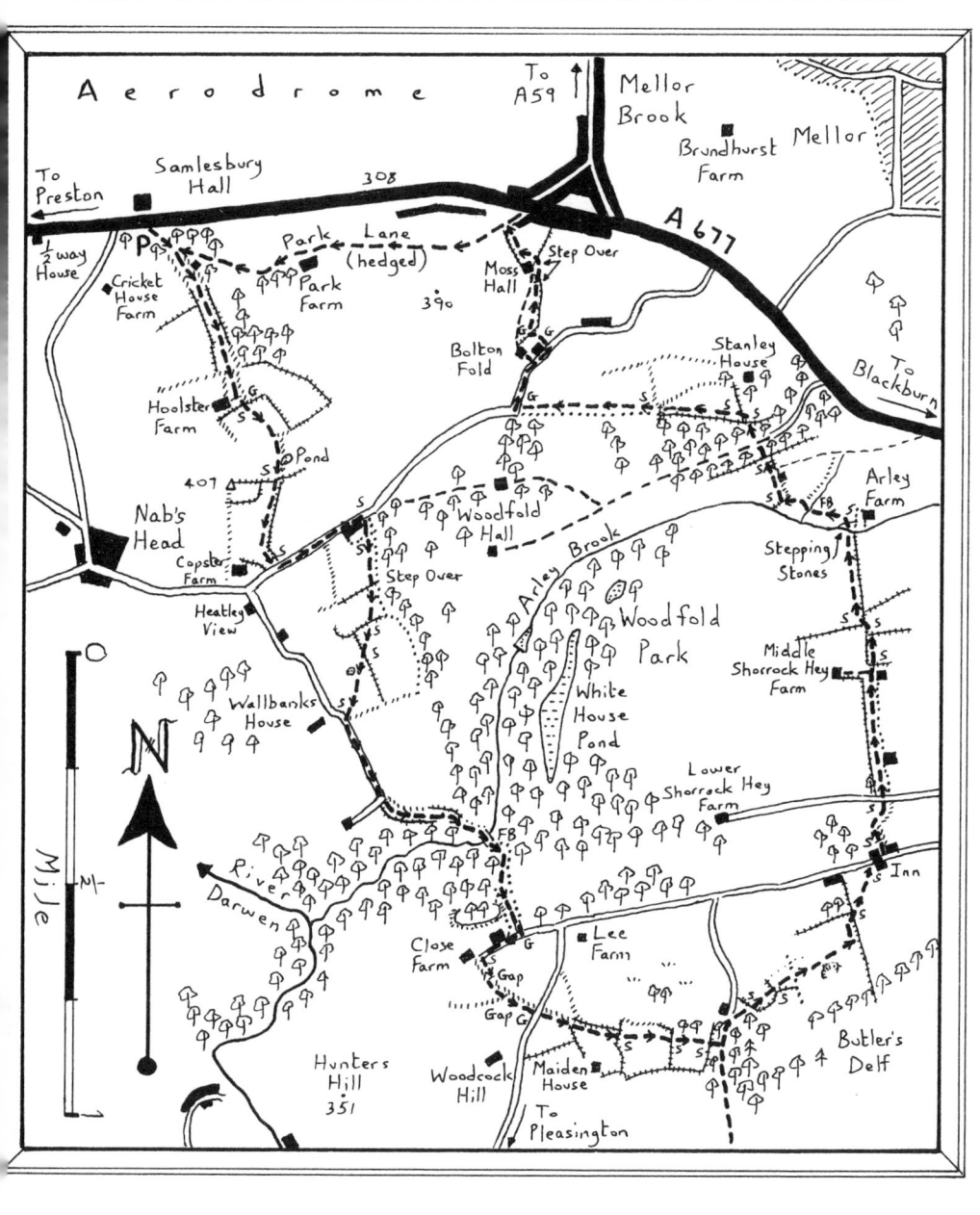

up the far side as the rough track slants above the tree line. Arriving at a gate, continue ahead on a metalled surface to a T-junction. Turn right towards Close Farm and take the first stile on the left immediately before the farm buildings. Follow a hedge until a gap is reached which allows you to continue on the far side all the way to a road. Cross straight over and along a track serving Maiden House. When this veers right, keep ahead with a fence/hedge on your left. Go over two stiles and then along an intermittent line of trees to the edge of some woodland.

This surrounds a dangerous quarry that is unseen on this walk but for which various signs give clear warning. Cross a stile into the trees and you will soon arrive at a T-junction. Bear left along the thin trod that soon merges with a wider track close to some houses. Opposite these, fork right up a grassy incline, go over a stile and then onto another over a fence before pursuing a gentle ascent of Butler's Delf. This is the highest point in the area and is marked by an abandoned quarry filled with water. Carry on to a fence and turn left along it to a stile. Thereafter descend a grass bank to the Blackburn road – adjacent to a pub.

Slant right and then left opposite the pub to go down a passage between houses. Cross a stile beside an electricity sub-station and follow the hedge on your right down to a farm road below. Go straight over and along a broad track heading north to its limit by some cottages. Step over a fence stile to continue downhill to a fence stile at the far side of the field. After this one, leap another on the left to gain the opposite side of the fence then continue down to the valley bottom where Arley Brook is crossed by means of some stepping stones. After another stile go alongside Arley Farm for only 50 metres before heading left along a trench.

At its far end, cross a narrow footbridge and stroll over to the field corner. Here cross a stile. Make your way to Lodge Wood up the right-hand edge of the next field beside a hedge. Keep a direct line through the wood to its far side then bear left along the top edge. Cross a fence stile and walk along to the next obstruction, a gap in the fence followed soon after by another stile.

Now accompany the wall to the edge of the woods and a gate that gives onto Further Lane. Lean right, passing the entrance to Bolton Fold. Immediately beyond the next house, ease through a slim gate on the left and along a fence. Keep left through a gap to reach the field behind. Go over to an iron-barred gate then down irregular grass pasture beside a hedge, homing in to a field corner. Beware of making contact with the 'lecky' fence, which offers a nasty jolt to loose appendages. Numerous bleeped epithets resulted from your intrepid guide being some-what careless in this respect.

Pass through a gate and circle right to reach the far side of Moss Hall, noting yet another of these unsociable barriers. Local landowners could at least provide appropriate stiles to retain the goodwill of those who have an age-old right to cross this land. Head down the access track at the far side to join Park Lane. This was once the main highway. Take a left along this hedged track which leads unerringly back to the start. As the crest of the route is gained, take note of any activity emanating from Samlesbury Aerodrome, which occupies the entire foreground on the right.

Walk 20. Osbaldeston

Remote Ribble's Haunted Halls

Mysteries: Oxendale Hall GR 651334;
Osbaldeston Hall GR 644344

Distance: 5 miles

Total Height Climbed: 250 feet (76 metres)

Nearest Shops: Mellor

Start and Finish: After turning left off the A59 at the Bay Horse Inn,
follow the narrow lane around to Osbaldeston Green. Park on
Osbaldeston Lane.

Map: Ordnance Survey 1:25 000 Explorer 19, West Pennine Moors

---

'If kindly peace be anywhere
'Tis surely here – 'tis surely here'

This pertinent observation epitomises the Ribble Valley once the main
road is abandoned. Narrow lanes harking back to a sedate age of gentil-
ity roll down to the banks of the river as it meanders in wide,
goose-necked loops across the valley bottomland. Gentle slopes
cloaked in a verdant tapestry of sombre woodland are set amidst bright
pastures and conceal deep cuttings where streams of some power have
eroded the soft clay terraces. Hidden from casual view, the walker suddenly finds himself thrust into an enclosed world of clinging vegetation
in contrast to the open fields and undulating pastures without. Tiny
hamlets boasting picturesque abodes clearly inhabited by those of ample means lie dotted across this rustic idyll.

It is evident from the lush greenery that heavy rainfall is no stranger
to the Ribble Valley, as I found to my cost recently. But what is a soaking
in the pursuit of walks of such quality and mystical allure?

The Walk

Having parked in Osbaldeston Lane, take a stroll up the access track
serving Roberts House Farm. Immediately before reaching the build-

ings, slant left and then keep left of a substantial hedge. Stick with this through a gap and then over a stile before reaching the road terminating at Oxendale Hall. Accompany the fenced road to the hall, where a solid gate discourages entry into the grounds. Presenting all the ingredients that go to make up the classic haunted house beloved of ghost writers, the sinister and macabre setting ought to offer us a host of frightening tales to chill the blood.

Oxendale Hall, where a phantom dog is said to roam.

No such luck! The current owner is unfortunately only able to pass on a suspicion that an elusive black dog visits the house. And like all such manifestations, it has been heard but never actually sighted. A nebulous chimera, this canine conundrum is rather a damp squib, if you will pardon the climatic analogy.

More relevant to walkers, however, is the mystery of the disappearing right of way that ought to take us to the right of Oxendale Hall, but appears to have been blocked off. Never fear though, there is an alternative passing between the new farm and the hall down to the tennis court. Then bear left and over a stile heading west along a fence.

After mounting another stile, cross an open field and go over a stile at the far side. Now lean half right, cutting across to a stile in the fence, and follow the hedge around to a batch of trees. A stile and footbridge will bring you out on a major access road serving Osbaldeston Hall – one of numerous rights of way that have been paved to the detriment of walkers.

Head towards the Ribble, the final 200 metres dropping quite steeply down to the baronial mansion below. On Sundays, the strident peel of bells echoing across the valley springs from the squat tower of Ribchester parish church. At one time, access to the far side of the river posed no problems as the right of passage included a ferry ride. Unfortunately, it was never replaced after destruction by fire. Anybody wishing to link up with the Ribble Way on the far shore will either have to bring their swimming togs, or head upstream for two miles to the nearest crossing point at Ribchester Bridge.

Osbaldeston Hall itself has been thoroughly refurbished in recent years, but even during its infancy in the 13th century was said to have 'eyries of hawks, hives of bees, cornmills and fisheries of great value'. Clearly it was intended to be self-sufficient at a time when the threat of invasion from marauders was rife.

Today a calm detachment belies a dark and sinister past when a heinous crime was perpetrated. During a family banquet, harsh words were exchanged between Thomas Osbaldeston and his brother-in-law. This later developed into a full-blown physical confrontation. Swords were drawn and a fierce duel enacted in which both combatants spilled much blood. Finally, Thomas slew his kinsman and blood from the fatal wound soaked deep into the floorboards. No amount of scrubbing was ever able to erase the gruesome stain, which is reputedly still visible to this day.

Visitors and residents have often heard cries and moans of agony filtering through the thick walls. Some have also perceived a fleeting wraith clutching a gory torso as it glides along the doleful corridors. According to the celebrated ghost hunter Peter Underwood, on a visit he made, 'the old house seemed to exude an atmosphere of unwelcome and brooding malevolence'. When I passed this way recently the only unwelcome elements in evidence were some rather noisy hounds. Could the obscure legend from Oxendale Hall have lost its way perhaps and ended up here? Or being ultra-sensitive to psychic phenomena, maybe these creatures had merely sensed a kindred spirit approaching.

Pass through the gate that gives access to the riverbank and head downstream. On reaching a fence barrier, take the left of two gates and follow the fence around the meandering edge of a large field. A pair of

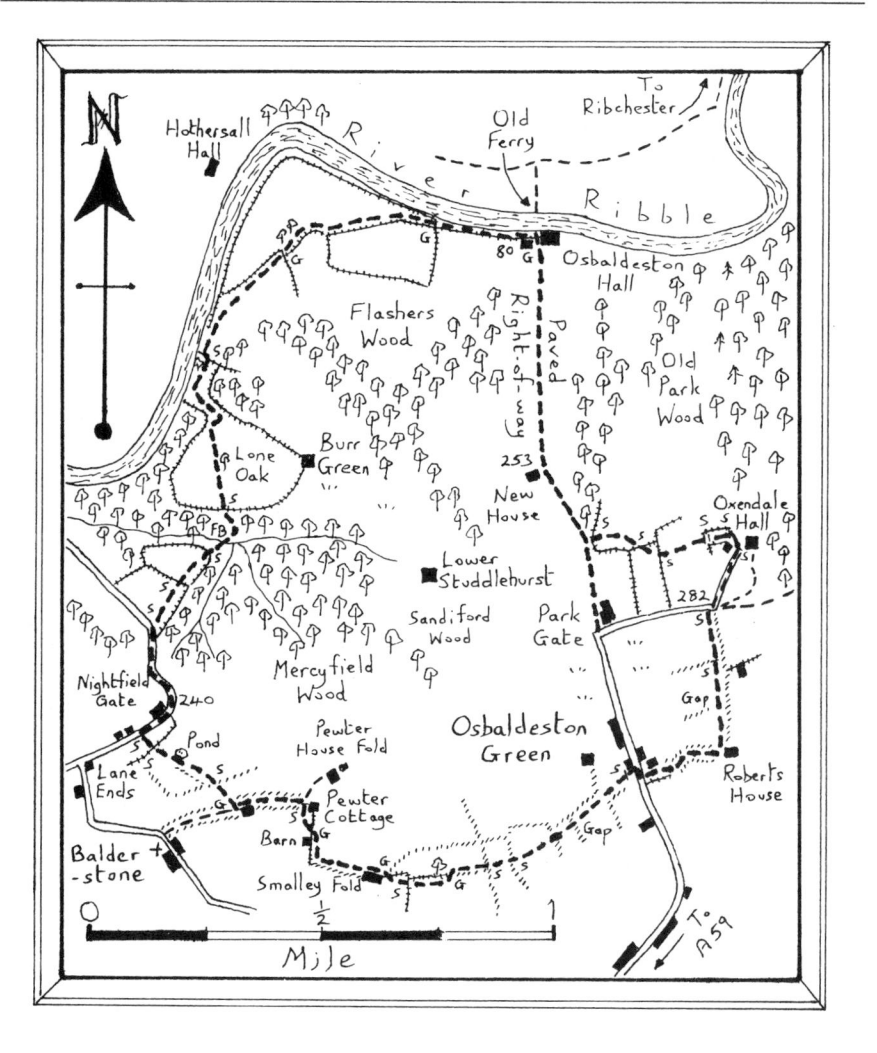

isolated gateposts should draw you in to join the fence and to a gate. Thereafter follow the fence, now on your right, along to a stile in some trees, heading towards the river's edge.

Cross a narrow brook before continuing along the riverbank for another 100 metres. Then bend left up the grassy rake between wooded tracts. At the top, cut back round the edge of the trees on the right until a grass corridor points the way to the far side of a cultivated field. Aim to pass beneath a lone oak as you make a beeline for Mercyfield Wood at the far side.

Pass through a stile and pick a tortuous course down into the enclosed cut. Go over a footbridge and up the far bank, which is stepped on either side. Exit via a fence stile, heading south along the tree line. Beyond another fence stile, continue on to join a back lane and slant left to pass Nightfield Gate. Stroll onward for another 100 metres, looking for a concealed stile in the thick hedge on the left.

After crossing a short stretch, mount a stile and head half left past a pond and along an intermittent hedge to a stile in a more substantial field boundary. Cross the next field, passing through a gate opposite an old house. Take a left up a broad, hedged track to Pewter Cottage. Go over a stile on the right of the cottage and work your way along to a gate adjacent to a barn. Keep to the edge of the field, passing behind Smalley Fold. At the far side, take the right-hand gate and walk along the right side of a fence. Cross a fence stile then, immediately beyond a tree-fringed pond, continue on the far side of a hedge by going through a gate.

A stile at the far end is followed by another in the fence on the right side of the next field. Now keep left of a pond, aiming for the far-left corner where a stile hidden by the hedge enables onward progress to be continued. Stroll along the hedge and through a gap until it veers sharp left. Keep going beside an intermittent hedge to reach the back gardens of the houses along Osbaldeston Lane. Cross a fence stile and walk along a grass corridor, thus returning to where you have left the car.

There are few walkers along this section of the Ribble Valley so paths are frequently intermittent. Such a dearth of like-minded individuals only serves to enhance the mysterious nature of the walk and is, therefore, to be relished.

Walk 21. Bashall Eaves

Red for Danger!

Mystery: The Red Pump Inn GR 696432

Distance: 4 miles

Total Height Climbed: 250 feet (76 metres)

Nearest Shops: Waddington

Start and Finish: In Bashall Eaves parking is limited to roadside verges, the most convenient being close to the right of way for Mason Green, which was once an ale house but is now a farm. The track is located midway between the village and the Red Pump Inn. Alternatively, have lunch at the pub and use its car park then digest the meal on this walk.

Map: Ordnance Survey 1:25 000 Outdoor Leisure 41, Forest of Bowland & Ribblesdale

---

Easily passed in the blink of an eye, the picturesque village of Bashall Eaves is delighted to have been voted the 'Best Kept Village' for 1991, a commemorative plaque being proudly displayed on the post office wall. But it is the pub that has received most attention, its renown even earning a personal notation on the Ordnance Survey map.

Built in 1756, the Red Pump Inn cannot be ignored. Its array of pumps are painted in the requisite hue, along with the window frames. Mystery and intrigue ooze from every pore of the building and it is well worth more than a cursory visit. Certainly the most bizarre incident to have dogged successive landlords came to light only recently when a strange square stone was unearthed during some building work. A goat's skull with ears of corn was carved into one side. When put on display for all to see, those who regularly came within its influence felt distinctly uncomfortable, the chilly hand of doom causing unexplained shivers.

Was it the 'Devil's Curse' that caused so many staff to fall ill, or mere coincidence? Whatever the origins of the mystic stone, it was returned to the earth from whence it emerged. The landlord in 1991 thought the stone would make an excellent advertisement for the inn and he accorded it a prominent position in the bar. But within 18 months he was forced to sell up and leave due to financial difficulties and the stone was sold to a medical consultant. If any reader knows of its whereabouts today, the best advice is to stay well clear.

An impish sprite that haunted the inn was said to be that of a young girl who lived there when it was a farm. Although a medium claimed her appearance indicated approval that the building was being well maintained, such visitations were exceedingly hard on the nervous system. A sprig of rosemary hung in a strategic position was sufficient to neutralise the ghostly effects.

In 1934 John Dawson was returning to his farm after an evening spent at the Red Pump when he felt a heavy thump in the back. Thinking some local hooligans had thrown a stone; he ignored the taunt and carried on to his home. During the night his shoulder became exceedingly painful and his wife called for an ambulance which took him to Blackburn Hospital. Three days later, the poor man was dead. It was found that he had, in fact, been wounded by a large bullet, but the subsequent police investigation could reveal no clues as to the culprit's identity. And to this day it remains an unsolved murder. Sometimes the squat figure of what is thought to be John Dawson is seen in the vicinity of the pub searching for the weapon that killed him. Bloodstains are clearly visible on his jacket.

The Walk

As you walk up the road to the village proper, take note of the Lancashire cheese press in front of the small cluster of cottages that fringe the green. It's an identical replica of how this most toothsome of local delicacies was produced. Continue past the post office, following the route taken by the Pendle Witches on their fateful journey to Lancaster Castle.

Cheese pressing at Bashall Eaves

After a quarter of a mile, fork left down a track and into a farmyard. On the gatepost note the unusual method used to keep track of the fishermen using this way to reach the River Hodder. Keep left of the buildings through a gate and stroll along the clear track that eventually terminates at a fence gate adjacent to Sandal Holme Farm.

The track continues beyond on grass to the edge of the downfall overlooking the Hodder. Bear left towards the lower section of woodland, where a fence stile is crossed. Lean right to walk along the tree-lined riverbank until an abrupt collapse of the pathway is reached. Here. a tributary cutting down from the left has caused instability of the earthen flanks on this side of the valley. Cross a fence stile on your right and drop down to ford the stream then go up a flight of steps on the far side to recross the fence. Climb an exceedingly muddy slope, slanting over to a fence stile on firmer ground.

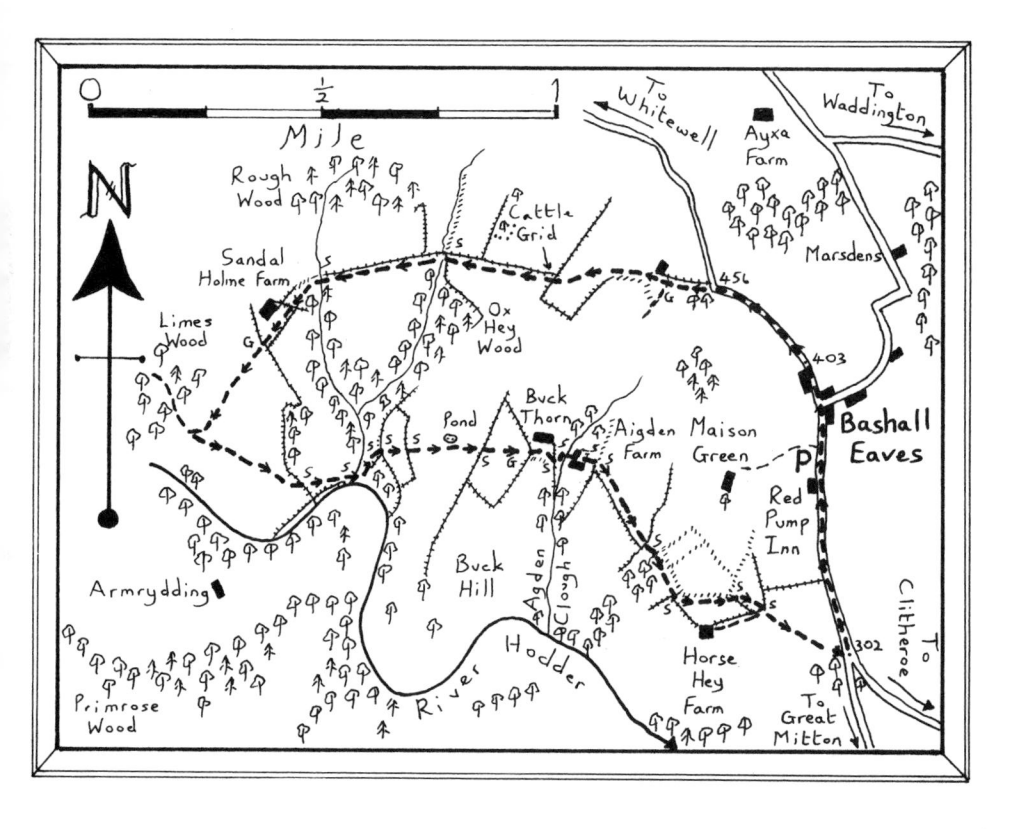

Here a deviation to the old right of way with stepped footings avoids what has become a dangerous mudslide. Meander up through the tree cover to emerge on a field above. Then head due east across level ground, passing an isolated stile (July 1998) after 50 metres. Maintain a straight course and pass right of a tree-girt pond. Go over a fence stile and across another field to arrive at Buck Thorn.

Once through the gate, keep right alongside a hedge to the periphery of dense woodland. After crossing a stile, a neat path winds its way down into the enclosed cutting of Agden Clough. Make use of the block stepping stones to cross the stream and go up the far side, veering left along a hedge to reach Aigden Farm. Pass straight through the farm-yard, which has a stile at either end, maintaining an easterly course. Cross over a short field section and through a hedge stile to accompany a fence on your right over two more fields. Straddling the next stile, the route crosses a short, open pasture to the fence opposite.

Now heading south-east with a hedge on your left, arrive at an over-grown corner with a broken stile to the right of a short piece of fencing. Slant left along a hedge to another old stile with a footbridge spanning a minor brook. Then bear half left across the field to join the access track serving Horse Hey Farm. Follow this back to a road junction and head left back to Bashall Eaves.

While passing the Red Pump, watch out for a strange character who may be preoccupied with solving his own demise. Could it be John Dawson? No reason to worry, unless of course he pays you more than just a passing glance.

Walk 22. Brungerley Bridge

All's 'Well' with the Devil

Mysteries: Brungerley Bridge GR 739429; Peg o' Nell GR 736426

Distance: 7 miles

Total Height Climbed: 250 feet (76 metres)

Nearest Shops: Clitheroe

Start and Finish: Take the B6478 out of Clitheroe towards Waddington, crossing the River Ribble by Brungerley Bridge. Park in a lay-by on the right, 100 metres beyond the bridge.

Map: Ordnance Survey 1:25 000 Outdoor Leisure 41, Forest of Bowland & Ribblesdale

Our walk begins on the Clitheroe side of Brungerley Bridge by passing through a gap in the parapet to descend a flight of stone steps and go over a small footbridge to gain the river bank. A solid structure, the first bridge erected in 1801 replaced a set of ancient stepping stones called The Hippings after a dam was built downstream to aid the cotton mills of Clitheroe. When the water level is low, it is still possible to discern the stones beneath the present bridge dating from 1816. This was the point where the Talbots of Bashall Hall, who were Yorkist sympathisers during the Wars of the Roses, captured Henry VI. Knowing this was the only spot where the rebel king could negotiate the River Ribble, they laid an ambush. He was then taken to London and incarcerated in the Tower. Rumour suggests that on learning his hideout at Waddington Hall had been discovered, Henry left in such a hurry that his dinner was only half eaten.

As with most river crossing points, there was an inn close by for the convenience of travellers. Here lived a tailor with a weakness for the hard stuff, a failing that had reduced him to an abject state of poverty. Such a situation was ripe for exploitation by Old Nick's manipulative connivance. By recounting a mystic spell, the poor tailor was promised great wealth. Although worried by the Devil's ultimatum, he nonetheless succumbed to the schemer's bargain. In exchange for three wishes,

The ancient and mystical crossing point of Brungerley Bridge

he would give his soul to the Devil twenty years hence. The first two wishes were thoughtlessly wasted. After confessing the deal to his wife, she exhorted him to seek advice from the Abbot of Whalley Abbey. Fearing a charge of devil-worship, he declined, and soon after the third wish was frittered away in like manner.

So distraught was the tailor at what he had done that he consulted the enigmatic Hermit of Pendle who persuaded him to adopt a more temperate and industrious lifestyle. This he duly did until the Devil eventually returned to claim his due. Hoping to discredit His Satanic Majesty on account of his lack of success in the wishing stakes, the tailor rigorously castigated the Devil's prowess. This was no idle tactic; there was indeed method behind this verbal challenge. In reply, Old Scratch stated that he would grant one more wish to prove his superiority. Nearby stood a dun horse chewing on the grass.

'I wish thou wert galloping into Hell upon yonder dun horse, never to return to plague poor mortals,' announced the tailor. Realising too late that he had been thwarted, the Devil was soon a speck on the distant horizon on his way back to the fiery portals of Hades. But never to return? History has proved on many occasions that his noxious influence is still felt.

The Walk

After trying to see the elusive Hipping Stones, make your way downstream until you reach a riverside wood and the first stile. Opposite, secured inside a small fenced enclosure, is Peg o' Nell's Well. The young lady in question worked at Waddow Hall. The Girl Guides Association now administers the stately home above the grass bank to the rear.

Of the various legends that surround the mysterious Peg, the most appealing concerns her caustic relationship with the lady of the house. Mistress Starkie frequently vented her irritation on the simple wench by giving Peg the most odious of tasks to perform. On one particular occasion, she sent Peg down to the well on a cold day when the ground was frozen solid. Little did she realise her waspish asides would result in the poor girl slipping into the river where she drowned in the icy ferment.

Eaten up with remorse, Mistress Starkie had a statue erected beside the well to the girl's memory. It was some time later that a clergyman was late arriving for an appointment at Waddow Hall. On learning that he had drowned whilst crossing the Hipping Stones, the lady blamed the recalcitrant spirit of Peg o' Nell. Belief in witchcraft, ghosts and the Devil was endemic at all levels of society in those ignorant times. She immediately took an axe to the statue and lopped off its head. Henceforth, all types of accidents and mischief in the district were blamed on Peg. Worst of all, it was claimed she was responsible for a death by drowning every seven years.

Ensure that this is not your unlucky year by hurrying up the stepped incline beyond the stile. Emerging onto a terrace above the river, follow a worn path through the grass to a stile. An enclosed track providing access to allotment gardens eventually brings you into a new housing development. Pass through and onto an extensive playing field, aiming left of the sports complex to gain the B6243. Turn right towards Longridge, soon crossing Edisford Bridge. Another primeval crossing point of the Ribble, it is renowned locally for a Norman defeat by Scots raiders back in 1137 when it was merely a ford.

Increased traffic from Lancaster by way of the Trough of Bowland led to the bridge being built. The identification marks of the stonemasons, who carved their personal logos into the parapet and arch supports, are unusual. Stroll up the rise on the far side of the river and take the side lane immediately past the Edisford Arms on the right.

After 100 metres, go over a stile in the hedge on the right and make a diagonal crossing of this long, narrow field. At its far corner beyond a small copse, cross a stile and accompany the fence now on your left to the access road serving Cheetall. Continue straight over and follow the right-hand hedge until it slants away as a fence. Carry on down to a stile at the far side of the field. After crossing a small fenced stream through a gap, keep ahead, mounting a fenced stile then proceeding through a line of trees to reach Twitter Lane.

A quarter mile down to the left is Bashall Town, a somewhat ambitious title as the settlement is barely worthy of hamlet status. Angle slightly to the left to locate a stile in the hedge on the opposite side of the road. Fork half left down to a gate adjoining the grounds of Bashall Hall. Once a prominent stronghold of the Talbot family who were fiercely loyal to the Yorkist cause in the 15th century, the ancient pile has been restored to its former glory behind the retaining wall. It was built to withstand all manner of assaults and has separate quarters provided for the private army that was always kept in readiness for battle.

After peeping into this unique aspect of Bashall's turbulent past, cross the stone footbridge and accompany a field track connecting the hall with Cow Hey. Entering the farmyard, bear left through a gate and follow the fence to its conclusion. Once over a stile, walk along the right bank of Bashall Brook to a new fence where a stile is crossed.

Chaperone the beck along a clear track until you reach the farm buildings of Clough Bottom and pass through a gate on the right. Heading north-east, nudge a fence corner and walk along some new conifer plantings to another gate. Thereafter, keep the fence on your left across two fields, maintaining a direct course when the fence disappears.

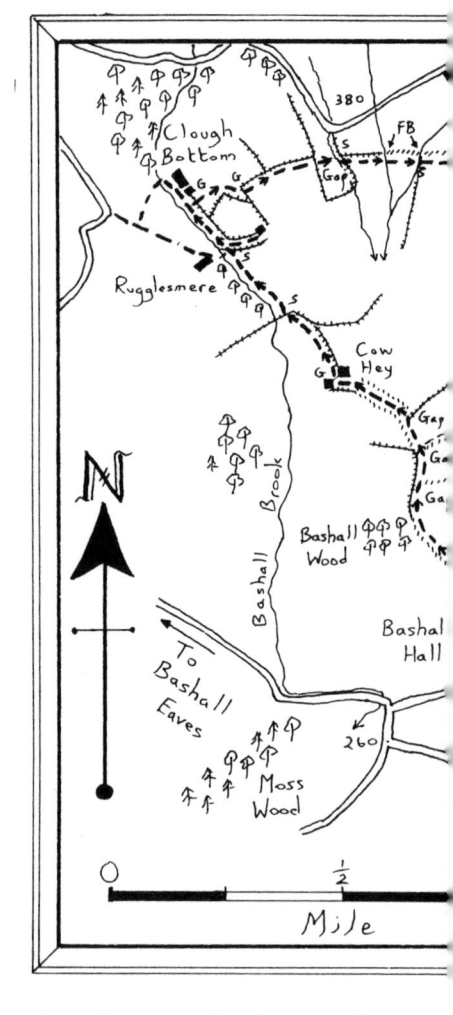

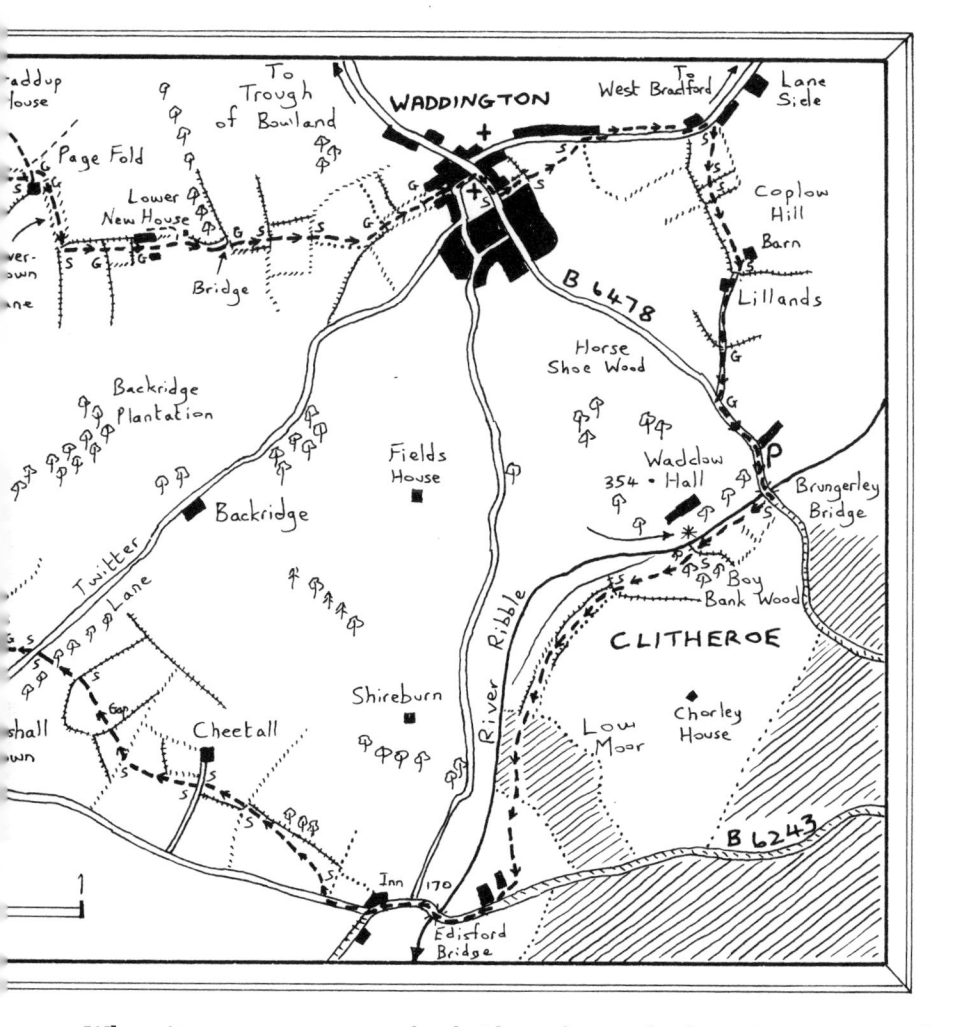

When it resumes, cross a footbridge where a hedge takes over – and soon another.

Keep on this easterly bearing all the way to Page Fold. The stile is tucked away in the left corner, hidden by some old farm machinery. Once on the farm access lane, take the gate opposite. Bend right through another gate to enter a constricted alley that is overgrown for much of its 300 metres. At the end, cross a stile and head left along a fence to enter the farm pasture of Lower New House. Pass the farm buildings and lean right, down to a substantial stone field-connecting bridge. Go through the gate on the left and follow the edge over three fields, which will bring you to a gate and a hedged track. Soon after, it becomes metalled and funnels into the village of Waddington.

Take time to assimilate the heady atmosphere of this prize-winning village. Beyond St Helen's Church, bear right down the main street, paying close attention to the superbly tended gardens that line the babbling brook. Even a novice gardener such as myself had to admire the diligent efforts of the villagers.

Immediately past Waddington Hall (where Henry VI once stayed), a stile points the way along a narrow passage between gardens, eventually opening onto a large field at the rear. Cross to the far right corner where a stile gives onto the West Bradford road. Head right for a quarter of a mile until a footpath signpost is reached just beyond the primary school. Now head due south across the field and over two stiles homing, into a fenced brook. Accompany this to a barn, after which a metalled road is joined that serves the isolated dwelling of Lillands. Stroll along this back to the B6478 then head left back towards Brungerley Bridge.

Walk 23. Pendle Hill

The Roof of Lancashire

Mystery: Pendle Hill GR 805414

Distance: 4½ miles

Total Height Climbed: 1100 feet (335 metres)

Nearest Shops: Downham

Start and Finish: One mile south-east of Downham on Pendle Road. Use a pull-in just beyond Hookcliffe Plantation on the right.

Map: Ordnance Survey 1:25 000 Outdoor Leisure 41, Forest of Bowland & Ribblesdale

---

No walking guide worth its salt can fail to include a visit to Pendle Hill. Indeed, it is impossible to ignore the whale-backed 'roof of the county' as it dominates the view in all directions. Although just short of the magical 2000ft which would automatically confer mountain status, Pendle Hill overshadows all other pretenders to his lofty throne.

Since time immemorial this giant has attracted a host of devotees, all seeking to bend the mountain (for mountain it surely is in the minds of all those within its realm) to their will. Like moths to a flame, visitors flock from far and wide to bear homage to Lancashire's crowning glory. Many camp up here on warm summer nights to witness a classic sunrise over the eastern horizon of the Pennines.

One of the most celebrated of pilgrims to walk the tough moorland grass and assimilate the latent aura of mystery surrounding Pendle Hill was George Fox. Like Jesus before him, Fox had sought to go out into the wilderness in search of his visionary calling. Soon after his release from Derby Gaol, where he had been imprisoned for blasphemy, he arrived in East Lancashire. George Fox's mission to spearhead a new enlightened Christian movement resulted in the creation of the Society of Friends or Quakers. Much persecution was to follow, but Fox always held firmly to his beliefs, sustained by the spiritual uplift he had imbibed on his visit to Pendle Hill.

Surveying the huge mammoth of Pendle towering over everything,

Enchanting Pendle Hill holds a fascination for walkers

he 'was moved of the Lord to go to the top of it; which I did, with much ado, it was so very steep and high.' He had clearly not yet toured the Lake District. But even if Pendle lacks the overall stature of a Scafell Pike, there can be no denying its influence on weather patterns in the area. A saying often referred to by locals has more than a hint of truth behind it,

> *'If Pendle's head do wear a hood*
> *Be sure the day will ne'er do good.'*

Numerous fissures and ravines that scar the lean slopes of Pendle's bulky torso, known locally as cloughs, are the result of subterranean reservoirs that have burst forth from the cracked façade at irregular intervals. Waters long pent up inside the grumbling bowels have caused havoc in surrounding villages.

One such event occurred on a stifling August day in the year 1580 when a torrential downpour resulted in unparalleled devastation. The floods were of such ferocity that bridges and houses were swept away. Although it only lasted for an hour, both human and animal life perished and many were left homeless. Such catastrophes are thankfully rare events.

Most of those who struggle up the steep gradient, particularly those of tender years, will no doubt be hoping for a glimpse of broom-flyers whizzing around the bleak summit plateau. For it is the 'bewitching' aspect of Pendle that is most remembered. Frightening tales of ugly harridans sitting round a campfire on Big End, stirring up a cauldron of spells, were sufficient to ensure that a young sprout of ten years stayed well away from the infamous site. Only recently in middle age have I chosen to make my first ascent. Witchcraft might well be the element that has brought notoriety to the hill, but we must journey south-east into Pendle Forest itself to uncover the sinister truth of the matter. And that must wait for Walk 24.

The Walk

This is probably the best circuit of Pendle Hill for clock-watchers as it is easily accomplished in an afternoon. From the pull-in, pass through a fence stile and up a rising path. After mounting a wall stile the moorland levels off, the path surging ahead across Downham Moor towards the acclivitous northern flank of the hill.

Cross a fence stile and follow a thin trod, initially veering left before making use of a series of deep grooves that zigzag up the steep grass bank. As the gradient eases the path bends right, crossing to the parish boundary wall. Beyond the ladder stile, head south to the top of Pendle Hill – generally referred to as Big End.

After 100 metres the path merges with the more popular Pendle Way and so up to the white trig column set on a gritstone circular base. But it is the extensive views that catch the eye, unless of course the date is October 31st. Then who knows? For the rest of the year, admire the bright green patchwork of fields that clothe the Ribble Valley, supported by the roller-coaster backdrop of the Bowland Fells behind.

To the east, the Forest of Pendle blends into the East Lancashire conurbation centred on Burnley. Continue south from the summit down a broad stony track for half a mile. Follow this until it circles left, descending the steep eastern flank on a clear path. Forking in towards the in-take wall close to Pendle House, pass through a stile at the bottom and walk along the side of a wall to a gate giving onto the access road.

Take a left to join a paved pathway that parallels the farm road. Continue down to Barley Lane then head left for 200 metres. Here the road swings right. Leave the road by crossing a wall stile on the left and accompany another wall over Pike Law to the field corner. Beyond this stile, the path picks a direct course through dense beds of reeds with

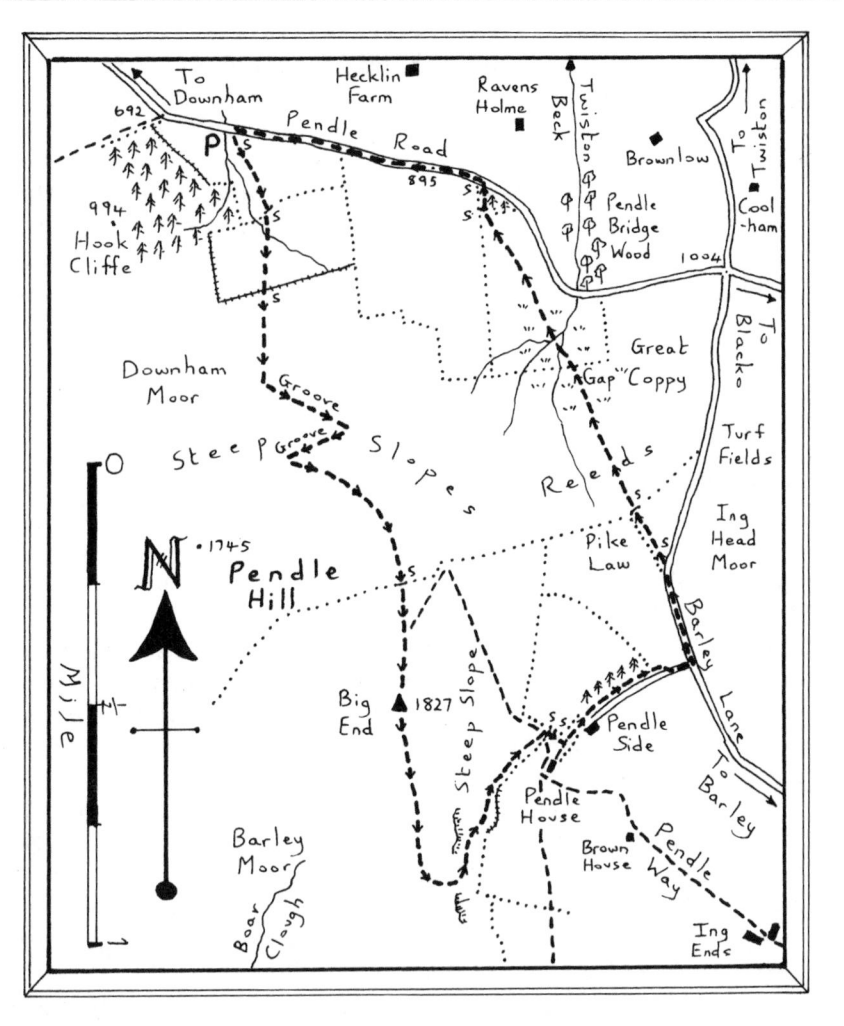

marker posts indicating the way. Drop down into marshy terrain that forms the drainage basin of Twiston Beck. Aim for a white-topped post indicating where the broken wall is to be crossed. Make your way over the various small rills and up the far side, keeping to a general north-westerly bearing when the path disappears.

This will soon bring you to a corner where walls merge and a stile is crossed into a new planting of conifers. Follow a thin path down the side of the wall to join Pendle Road. Head left for less than one mile on a downward slant back to the car pull-in.

Walk 24. Pendle Forest

Bewitching!

Mysteries: Roughlee Hall GR 844404;
Lower Well Head GR 817390; The Eye of God GR 823394

Distance: 5½ miles

Total Height Climbed: 600 feet (183 metres)

Nearest Shops: Barley

Start and Finish: Park on the right side of the road as you climb
out of Newchurch-in-Pendle.

Map: Ordnance Survey 1:25 000 Outdoor Leisure 41, Forest of
Bowland & Ribblesdale

Before you can even begin to unravel the mysteries secreted within the
'Witch Country' of Pendle Forest, it is necessary to actually get there.
With this vital aspect in mind, ensure that you have a suitable road atlas
close to hand. Your sagacious guide was not so astute and found himself
completely lost on more than one occasion. It is easy to lose your bear-
ings along narrow lanes that twist and turn across these undulating
hills of East Lancashire.

Being a hunting ground of royal patronage during the Middle Ages,
the actual forest covered little more than is evident today. Tiny hamlets
and villages hidden within the folds of the switchback landscape have
long harboured prejudice and superstition that have brought a degree of
infamy that none at the time could have imagined. Tales of witchcraft
and devilish intrigue draw visitors from far afield into this turbulent
outpost of the county. But the very nature of the hilly terrain also encouraged the practice of highway robbery due to the ease with which
felons could evade the clutches of the law. The infamous Kirk Gang,
who frequented the lonely trails of Pendle Forest, is known to have hidden its booty under the flat stones to be found in the graveyard of St
Mary's at Newchurch.

Once known as Goldshaw Booth, the newly created church in the
15th century led to the change of name. And Newchurch, ranging up

Meet the witches of Newchurch-in-Pendle

the north flank of the valley, has acquired a reputation as the focus for the witchcraft that is no idle legend to be derided out of hand. Indeed, three of the frightful harridans that terrorised the district are seated outside the only remaining village shop. Give them a wide berth lest spells of evil intent be cast.

The Walk

Our walk begins by taking the footpath heading east from the road above Newchurch towards Barley Bank Wood. Enter it over a wall stile and slant half left along a straight path between sombre ranks of dominant conifer, stepping over a carpet of pine needles. Mount a low wall in the middle of the wood and exit at the far side, bearing left to join a wall. At the end of a conifer plantation, climb a double stile to gain the far side of the wall then continue onward to Heys Lane. Cross straight over this rough-walled track, dropping down to meet a back lane close to the hamlet of Thorney Holme.

On the left opposite is an access lane serving White Hough. Stroll down this to cross a bridged tributary and turn immediately left alongside until a signpost nudges you right in the direction of the outdoor education centre. Follow the narrow lane between a close of stone houses and up the far side of the vale until a small brick building is reached on the right. Sandwiched between this and a holly tree is a stile that allows passage through the wooded enclave adjoining the centre. Accompany the thin trod which crosses a small footbridge just before leaving the wood by a fence stile. Bear left along the edge of the trees to Intake Farm, where a stile and gate allow movement through the farmyard and down the access track.

Cross straight over the back lane to mount a fence stile and so cross a field. Midway lies a dual fence followed soon after by another in a hedge close to Croft House. Now lean right and cross a fence stile heading south-east over the fields towards Roughlee.

Keep a direct course over a footbridge followed by a fence stile then home in to join a hedge. Follow this down to a gate on the edge of the village. Walk along a narrow track to gain the lane paralleling Pendle Water. Take a right to arrive at Old Hall Close, where Roughlee Hall stands framed between upmarket residences – the juxtaposition of past and present in classical harmony.

This was the home of Alice Nutter, reputedly buried in the churchyard at Newchurch. Hanged in 1612 on Lancaster Moor along with others condemned for witchcraft, it would appear that she found herself in the wrong place at the wrong time. As a staunch Catholic, it is thought that she went to the 'witches' coven' at Malkin Tower thinking it was a clandestine meeting of the faithful and not to fraternise with the devil. Alice was clearly of high breeding, unlike the hideously depraved families who were forever causing mayhem in the vicinity. Known as Chattox and Demdike, their simple-minded actions included the casting of spells and consorting with 'familiars'. To the modern ear, it seems strange indeed that supposedly intelligent justices who administered the law in 17th-century England could have been taken in by the hocus-pocus of witchcraft.

Consider these mysterious events as you return to a stile on the right after which the path drops down to cross Pendle Water by a set of concrete bollards. Climb up the opposite bank aiming left for a post on the near horizon. From there, head directly uphill until a wall is reached.

The Pendle Way (marked along signposts hereabouts by a flying witch) continues onward to Barrowford in the next valley. Our route heads right to meet the brow of the road rising from Roughlee and provides the first sighting of Pendle's enigmatic dome (see Walk 24) which contrasts markedly with urban development in the Calder Valley.

Continue heading south-west up the access road, forking right to pass Ridgaling Farm. It then becomes a straight track between hedge and fence. On reaching a wall, maintain a direct course on the right of this all the way to Noggarth Cottage at the corner of Ridge Lane. Stop for a break at the café if the mood takes you then continue on for only 50 metres to mount a wall stile on the right. Make a left diagonal crossing of the field to a wall corner and slant away to cross a fence stile at the end. Return to the boundary line and keep going on the right of a fence to another stile.

Now cross to the far side of a walled corner and go over the next field, aiming midway along the fence. Remember that we should eventually pass immediately left of the soaring radio mast ahead. After this stile, make a gradual ascent of the broad, grassy ridge. Pass through two broken walls before reaching the next real field boundary.

Beyond the stile, keep left of a fence for 100 metres then you cross to the far side and continue in the adjoining field. Pass right of Spen Height, crossing another fence stile as the walled enclosure of the pylon is approached. In the left corner is a stile allowing access to the track serving Higher Spen. Stick with this past the steel rig until a stile on the right enables you to cross a short field to gain the corner of Spenbrook Road as it drops down to the carpet factory. Bear left, taking note of a fence stile to be negotiated 50 metres on the right.

Cut over the field corner to reach the track to Tinedale Farm which circles left alongside a wall. Immediately beyond the farmhouse, mount a stile into a rough track (initially walled) that points the way to the far side of the valley and Bull Hole. The most exciting feature on this latter section of the walk is the isolated stone cottage of Lower Well Head sited on the rising slope ahead. It was here that Old Mother Demdike, a blind, eighty-year-old harridan, raised her disreputable brood in a hovel on the site known as Malkin Tower.

Originally thought to be a pele tower for defence against raiding brigands from the north, it was demolished soon after the witch trials in 1612 to obliterate all reference to this heathen crew. All that remained were the foundations, which were used for the current building of Lower Well Head.

It was Bessie Whittle of the Chattox clan who lit the touch paper by stealing clothes from Malkin Tower and wearing them to church. Charged with the theft, she countered by accusing the Demdikes of witchcraft. And all hell literally broke loose, the repercussions filtering down through the centuries and bringing fame of a dubious kind to Pendle Forest.

As you approach the walled track before Bull Hole, locate a stile on the right. Follow the fence now on your left over four more fence stiles to gain the far side of Moss End, the last enabling you to make use of a grass causeway over the middle of the adjoining field. Still maintaining a direct line aiming north-east, three more stiles will bring you to Spenbrook Road opposite Newchurch Primary School. Amble left, up the village street to visit the church of St Mary watched by the eye of God peering down at you from the old tower. Carved into the stonework, this religious symbol was intended as a protection for the congregation against evil influences occasioned by the Devil. Could it be that the architect had foreseen the ominous conflagration that was to inflame the hearts and minds of the populace some two centuries later?

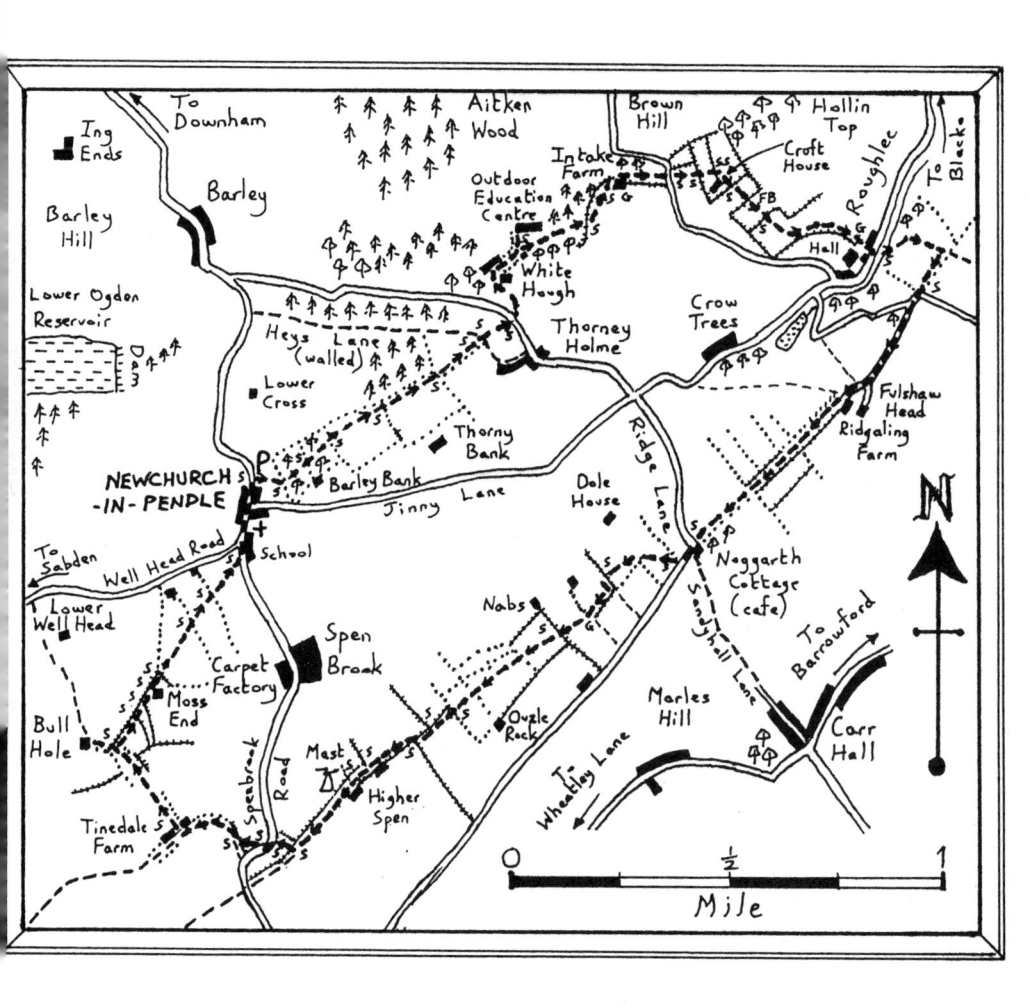

Walk 25. Rufford

Shake, Rattle and Shiver

Mysteries: Rufford Old Hall GR 463160; Black Bull Inn GR 498151; Mawdesley Hall GR 497151

Distance: 6 miles

Total Height Climbed: Nil

Nearest Shops: Rufford

Start and Finish: Make use of the railway car park sandwiched between the station and White Bridge at Rufford.

Map: Ordnance Survey 1:25 000 Pathfinder 699, Chorley and Burscough Bridge

Ensconced within a tall screen of leafy boughs, Rufford Old Hall is squeezed between the Leeds-Liverpool Canal and the busy A59 trunk road. Now administered by the National Trust, the hall boasts an impressive pedigree stretching back into the swirling mists of time. Heskeths have lived on this site since the 14th century although the current dwelling dates from the Tudor period.

The celebrated connection with a certain playwright of Elizabethan renown has long been claimed for Rufford, ensuring the hall's unique place in literary circles. It was here that the Hesketh Company of Players employed the talents of a young thespian by the name of William Shakeshafte to add a confident piquancy to their performance. Often referred to by this name, the 'Bard of Avon' had at the time felt it prudent to remove himself from the vicinity of Stratford when deer from the local forest went missing. Lord Strange of Rufford was more than willing to exploit the flair displayed by this rising star of the theatre in 1593. This astute decision effectively promoted the allure of Rufford Hall thereafter.

During the same period, it was mooted that Elizabeth I herself stayed at the hall. Although no records of such a visit have ever been found, ghostly sightings of the Virgin Queen have been witnessed in the large

Rufford Hall has eminent literary connections

dining room. When approached, the spectre fades into the oak panelling.

But perhaps the most well known of the mysterious 'drop-ins' is that of The Grey Lady who roams the grounds and corridors of Rufford Hall still dressed in her somewhat discoloured wedding gown. The story goes that prior to her marriage to one of the Hesketh nobles in the 16th century, the patriotic aristocrat was ordered to quell an uprising of insurgents who were raiding to the north. Anticipating his return, the lady sat by her window day after day. But he never came back, and eventually she died pining for a lost love that was never consummated. She steadfastly refused to discard the dress. Her appearances, it has to be said, are becoming a distinct rarity these days. The usual sign of a 'presence' can be the sudden drop in temperature or a chilling draught that traces a finger down your spine. Then you will, indeed, know The Grey Lady is close by.

The Walk

From the railway station car park, cross White Bridge and turn immediately left down the access track serving the rich and fertile agricultural plain of Mawdesley Moss. Stretching away into the distance, fields separated by drainage dykes grow all manner of vegetables for the supermarket shelves. On the day I passed this way, leeks and carrots were the chosen crops, the dark productive loam being ideal for large-scale cultivation.

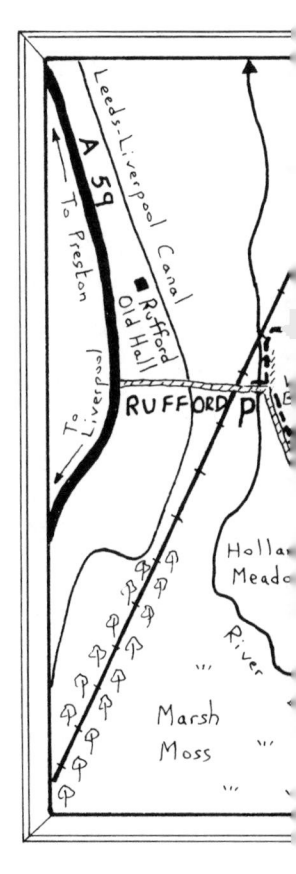

After 200 metres, the track bears right and should be followed until a wooden bridge is reached spanning The Sluice. Continue on the far side to the field corner and T-junction of dykes. Head left for 200 metres to the top end of the field. Now resume an easterly direction on a dead straight course along the edge of various fields until you arrive at an old ladder stile.

Go straight over a north/south field track known as Gales Lane until you arrive at a pair of young saplings. Lean to the right and follow the open field boundary, aiming for a white building in the middle distance. This is Boundary Farm where you should bear right along the track that links it to Cliffs Farm. Swing left through the farmyard, and at the far end take to the fields again. Now enclosed by hedging, cross to the far side through a gate and then head due south across a large grassy patch. Keep 100 metres right of Rectors Wood until you arrive at a gate giving on to a rough, hedged track.

Accompany it down to a gate then over a couple of stiles to reach a back lane with the Black Bull Inn on the right. Now a quiet country pub, it was once a hangout for local ruffians, with fierce brawls a regular feature of the Saturday night entertainment. Hence it became known as 'Hell Hob'. Revellers would sit round a roaring fire and boast of sitting on the 'Hob of Hell Fire'. A huge poker hanging by the side of the hearth and weighing in at sixteen pounds was used to stoke up Old Nick's mischief and bets were placed on who could wield it with most dexterity. One landlord claimed to have imprisoned in a bottle the spirit of an old woman who haunted nearby Mawdesley Hall, his aim being to attract more custom to his drinking den. But fearing that the potent influence of the incarcerated phantom might rebound onto him, the superstitious host threw the bottle into a pit where it still resides.

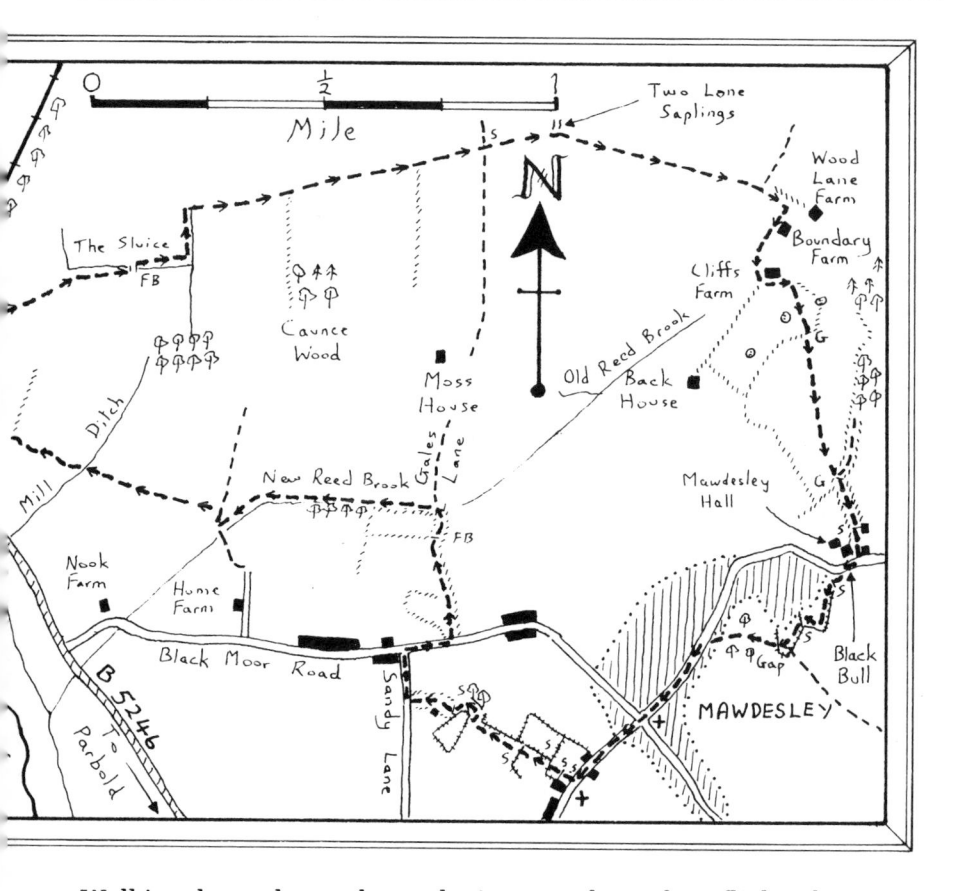

Walking down the road past the inn, watch out for a flight of steps cut into the rock on the right. Ascend these for an impressive view of the half-timbered farming residence of Mawdesley Hall dating back to 1625.

Continue down the road and bear left opposite the war memorial. Slant immediately right to mount a fence stile and climb a short rise alongside the fence on your left. Keep with this around the edge of the field until a stile and footbridge are reached adjoining a new housing development. Stroll past the houses to a children's playground at the end. Pass through the fence gap on the far side, taking a tortuous path through scattered dwarf oaks to emerge on the main street of Mawdesley village. Bear left down to the crossroads of Four Lane Ends.

On the opposite corner is Finch Cottage – named after the family who kept the preserved skull of a distant relative in a hidden chapel.

These were the only remains of William Haydock, a Catholic monk executed in 1536 for his contrary beliefs. Mary Haydock was the descendant who brought the relic to Mawdsley after marrying Thomas Finch, and here they created the chapel that became a shrine on account of the skull's healing properties. A similar fate befell a relative of William Haydock – see Walk 14.

Continue over the crossroads and past the village school for 200 metres and take a narrow, signposted passage on the right with a stile at either end. Follow the fence on your left and over the next stile, after which the fence is on the right. Climb another and stroll on until you arrive at a fenced diversion around the edge of the field. You have now reached the last stile on this particular walk. Mount it and walk along the hedged corridor beyond down to Sandy Lane. Bear right to Black Moor Road and right again for 100 metres until a gap on the left points the way across the moss land.

Follow a path along a tree-lined dyke for a quarter of a mile until it bends gradually right over a substantial flat bridge. Join Gales Lane, continuing north for a further 100 metres. At the next hedge, veer left along the edge of New Reed Brook and past a narrow strip of trees. The path soon crests an embankment overlooking the cultivated fields. When a major track is reached bear right along this for only 50 metres before heading left again on another clear track. Beyond Mill Ditch, carry on with a small dyke on your left towards a line of trees. Keep right of these until you arrive at the Parbold road, where a right will return you to White Bridge.

Walk 26. Croston

The Tainted Cross

Mysteries: Little Red Riding Hood GR 491183; The Sarscow Lady GR 504191

Distance: Short route – 4 miles. Longer route – 5½ miles

Total Height Climbed: Insignificant

Nearest Shops: Croston

Start and Finish: Unless you intend to make use of the facilities offered by the numerous hostelries in Croston, parking is limited to the main road close to the village centre.

Map: Ordnance Survey 1:25 000 Pathfinder 699, Chorley and Burscough Bridge

---

One of numerous 'dormitory' settlements that have expanded across the West Lancashire Plain in recent years, Croston is ideally situated for commuters working in any of the North-West's major cities. Nondescript housing almost swallows up the heart of this old village that grew up around its preaching cross. Although a modern addition carved from a millstone, the cross rests on a plinth dating back to Saxon times when missionaries would stop here to preach the word of God. It stands at the entrance to Church Street whose cobbled access to 17th-century brick cottages exudes a timeless appeal that no amount of contemporary growth can subdue.

This would have been an easy point to cross the River Yarrow, as the packhorse bridge dated 1682 appears to testify. Unfortunately, the river was frequently prone to bursting its banks before flood control measures were implemented to curb its potent zeal. Now sidling between steep walls, it is hard to imagine that this placid flow was capable of lapping against the back door of adjacent cottages.

Handloom weaving of flax was a major occupation in the 18th century until it declined when steam power transferred the booming textile industry into the local mills. The Liverpool/Preston railway further stimulated expansion; effectively bringing to an end the self-sufficient insularity that had characterised Croston for centuries. Today even the rustic ambience of Church Street and its environs has to be shared with that most ubiquitous symbol of modern England – the motor car.

The Walk

Take a stroll down to St Michael and All Angels Church and under the archway of the old schoolhouse to cross the Yarrow by a narrow footbridge. Turning immediately left will bring you into the cemetery. In keeping with many ancient settlements, Croston Cemetery possesses its very own ghost. It is said to be the spirit of a young girl who died in 1890, friendless and alone according to her epitaph.

Mary Hudson's grave lies forlorn and neglected in a corner of the cemetery where her spirit dressed in a red shawl was often seen by the village teacher. This was the uniform of the local children's home. So perhaps Little Red Riding Hood only wanted someone to offer her the warmth and kindness she failed to experience during her sad life. Certainly, this particular spectre is unlikely to harbour any malicious intent to those fortunate enough to witness a visitation.

Returning to the cross, bear left along the main street for 300 metres, continuing past the T-junction where the main road veers left. Swing right behind the primary school and along the edge of a football pitch. Keep close to the fenced rear of the houses on your left to enter a narrow passage that zigzags round to a gate adjoining an open field. Make a diagonal crossing to a ladder stile at the far side that brings you to the limit of a modern housing estate. Lean immediately right, down a fence/hedged passage that squirms round to join the B5249. Bear right for 200 metres then go over a stile to head north alongside a hedge.

At the end of the field, use a stile to continue on the opposite side of the hedge. Beyond the next stile, angle half right to the far corner and a gate close to where the River Lostock passes beneath Littlewood Bridge. Cross straight over the lane and continue along the riverbank, now heading east against the flow. After the first barrier, which turns out to be a stile hidden in the hedge close to the waterline, reach a footbridge and turn right along a fence, away from the river. Join a gravel track through a gate and stroll down to pass right of The Mill Hotel.

At its far side and sandwiched between the Royal Umpire Caravan Park lies Gradwells Farm. At one time in the not so distant past it was famous for the finest collection of horse-drawn carriages in the north of England. This has now sadly been dismantled. Less renowned but far more intriguing is the haunted element that has lingered around Gradwells since the 17th century.

At that period the owners were devout Catholics and many who lived here became priests. Due in no small measure to the degree of persecution suffered by those following the faith, a hide was constructed beneath the fireplace which was supposedly connected to St Michael's by a secret tunnel. In view of the distance involved, namely one mile as the crow flies (or more accurately as the mole burrows), this would seem to be an unlikely proposition. A cross erected in the garden is in memory of a priest by the name of Winckley, who resided at Gradwells. Could this be the same chaplain who fell in love with 'The Sarscow Lady'?

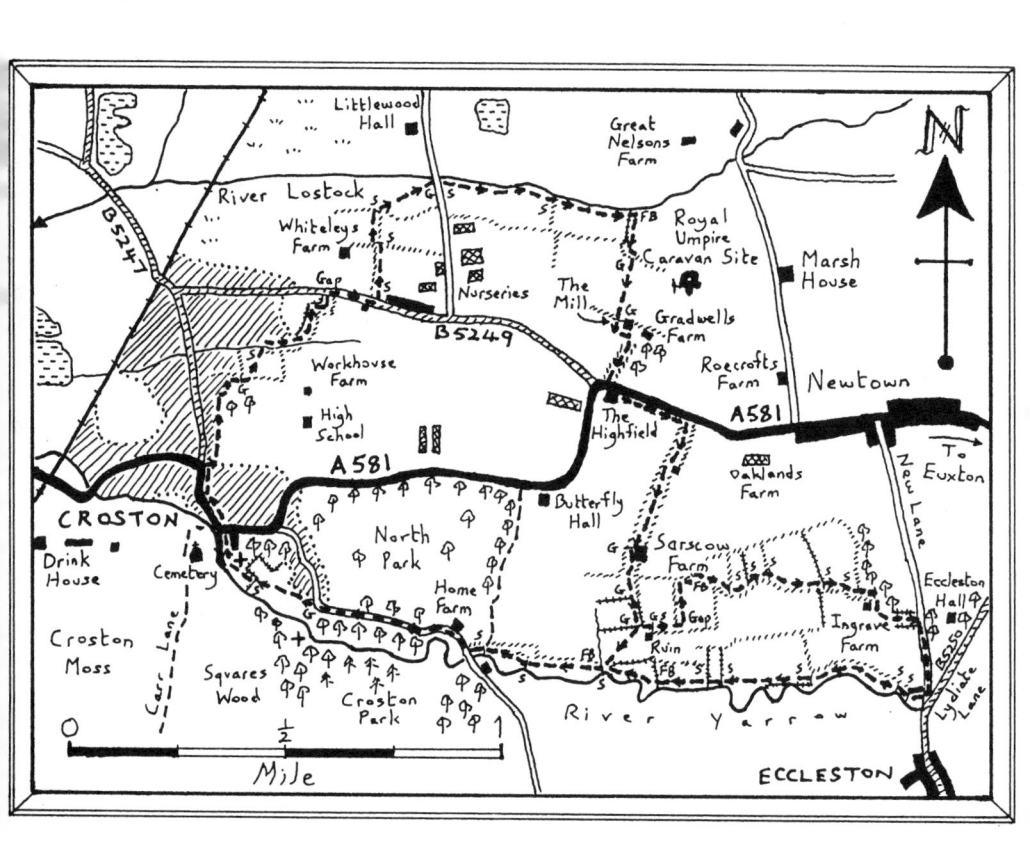

The story is told of a young girl from nearby Sarscow Farm who threw herself into the well behind Gradwells when her clerical lover died from the fever. Although nobody has ever actually seen her, numerous reports of shifting furniture, rustling garments and various unexplained noises testify that a haunting presence was abroad at Gradwells Farm. Since the cross was moved to a new spot in the front garden, the ghost would seem to have faded into the brickwork. But only four hours after the cross was repositioned, a bus driver refused to continue past the end of the access lane. He was convinced that he had knocked a woman down. Suffice it to say that no body was found. Maybe this was the final curtain for 'The Sarscow Lady'.

The 'Sons of Divine Providence' now run the farm and offer holidays to handicapped people. When questioned, they had no knowledge of their ephemeral guest who it would appear is still 'resting'. What it will take to resurrect her can only be surmised.

Leave this enchanting anomaly by strolling down the drive to a major junction and heading left for 300 metres until you reach Sarscow Lane. Head south down this rough, hedged track serving the farm where our elusive ghost once resided. Pass through a gate on the right and continue down an enclosed section that soon opens out with a hedge on the left. Two gates will bring you to a large field, and decision time!

Those lone walkers who suddenly remember it is their wedding anniversary should make a diagonal crossing to the far corner where a footbridge will deposit you on the bank of the River Yarrow. If your conscience is untroubled then head left through a gate to pass a ruin. Mount a fence stile and at the next gap bear left along a hedge.

At the field corner, follow the hedge round to a small footbridge, thus gaining the far side of Spent Brook. Keep going in an easterly direction over a stile and a new excavation for a gas main (October 1998). Hopefully by the time you come this way, the field will have been restored to its former grassy state. Three more stiles and you should arrive at a tree-lined passage. Overhung with a sylvan guard of honour, accompany it round to emerge onto the access track serving Ingrave Farm. At New Lane turn right and continue for a quarter of a mile, until Bridge Foot is reached. Lean right past the front door of this cottage on the bank of the River Yarrow and go along a short, hedged corridor.

Mount the stile at the end followed by another soon after and follow the river flow alongside an adjacent hedge. Watch out for the next stile, which takes you onto the opposite side of a fence. Maintain a straight course heading due west to cut off the snaking meanders of the Yarrow at this later stage of its development.

The next barrier is the gas main excavation with stiles at either side. Now accompany a straight section of the river over a footbridge before another wide loop. Keep on ahead to a fence stile adjoining the trees that conceal the footbridge on the right. This is the point where the shortened route is joined.

Slant away from the river along a hedge to another stile, thereafter continuing onward until the hedge circles left to enable us to join a major track downstream from the corn mill. Soon after, a lane is reached where we head right past Home Farm towards Croston.

Stroll along a tree-lined section until you reach the entrance to the Church of the Holy Cross. Just beyond this, open a small gate and cross the field behind some gardens. Aim for the riverbank and a fenced passage with a stile at this end only. This funnels you into the churchyard at the rear of St Michael's. Slowly amble down the cobbled thoroughfare of Church Street. All too soon, it merges with the main road and a different world entirely.

Croston affords a glimpse into the hazy past

Walk 27. Rivington

Follies

Mysteries: The Dovecot GR 640143; Rivington Pike GR 643138; The Castle GR 628131

Distance: 6 miles

Total Height Climbed: 1000 feet (305 metres)

Nearest Shops: Horwich

Start and Finish: Ample parking is available in Rivington Park. The most convenient for the start of this walk is in the car park behind Great House Barn, on the left side of Rivington Lane and opposite the access road to Rivington Hall Barn.

Map: Ordnance Survey 1:25 000 Explorer 19, West Pennine Moors

Famed throughout the county as the original country park, Rivington has become the playground of the north with reservoirs stacked up along the Goit Valley which have effectively turned the area into a miniature 'Lake District'. Set out under the tutelage of the late Viscount Leverhulme, the estate was acquired for the princely sum of £60,000 in 1899.

This 'lad from Bolton' made his mark and fortune in the household cleansing business and had a vision to develop an exotically orchestrated holding for the benefit of his hometown. In keeping with Victorian traits exhibited by the landed gentry, William Hesketh Lever employed expert gardeners and landscape architects to bring his dream to fruition. Rare plants and shrubs, waterfalls in quirky grottoes linked by a labyrinth of terraced footpaths adorned the rising flank beneath Rivington Moor. Without doubt, their design was much influenced by Lever's numerous foreign visits, particularly to Japan and Italy. Exploring the charming secrets of this quaintly archaic slice of Bolton heritage is, however, beyond the scope of this book.

As befitted an accomplished entrepreneur of the age, Viscount Leverhulme was a prodigious builder of that symbol intended to overtly flaunt power and wealth – the folly. Not one but two – namely, the

The Dovecot at the edge of Rivington Moor

Dovecot located high up on the edge of the moors, and Liverpool Castle sited on the east bank of Lower Rivington Reservoir.

It is perhaps significant that the most famous of them all was erected in 1733 by John Andrews. Prominent from all western approaches, eyes are automatically drawn to Rivington Pike, which presents the appearance of a giant pimple on the moorland torso. Only then are we inevitably tempted to ogle the towering radio mast atop Winter Hill (See Walk No.28).

Viscount Leverhulme made his name in soap and is best remembered for building Port Sunlight for the workers employed in his factories on the Wirral. A fitting link between the two places is the chain of reservoirs built in the mid-19th century with the express aim of supplying corporation pop to Liverpool, a function that is still in operation today.

The Walk

We begin our walk by strolling down through the trees to follow the lakeside path in a northerly direction. Approaching the causeway separating Upper and Lower Reservoirs, lean right alongside a fence to a car park. Pass the primary school, still housed in its original 18th-century building, and bear right to reach the village green with its water trough and stocks.

Of ancient origin, this is the heart of Rivington and boasts two churches. It is, however, largely overshadowed by more recent development associated with Country Park status. Just beyond Rivington Lane, pass through a stile on the left and follow a fence beyond a ruined farm down a flight of stone steps. After mounting another stile, the path accompanies a stream round to a major track serving Dean Wood House.

Climb steadily up to the top edge of the woods where a stile gives on to an open field. Bear right along the edge of the tree line until a stile is reached. Here the path switches to the opposite side and proceeds along a fenced corridor on the lip of a steep-sided ravine. Hemmed in with dense undergrowth, a stile at the end brings us out on a back lane. Head left for 50 metres towards Wilcock's Farm, then mount a ladder stile on the right, followed by another over the wall on the left. Walk east along the left edge of a narrow dyke until a stile is reached which will deposit you in a broad fence/wall corridor.

After 200 metres, the fence ends and a wall begins. On the approach to a huddle of conifers, slant right and through a gate to join Sheep

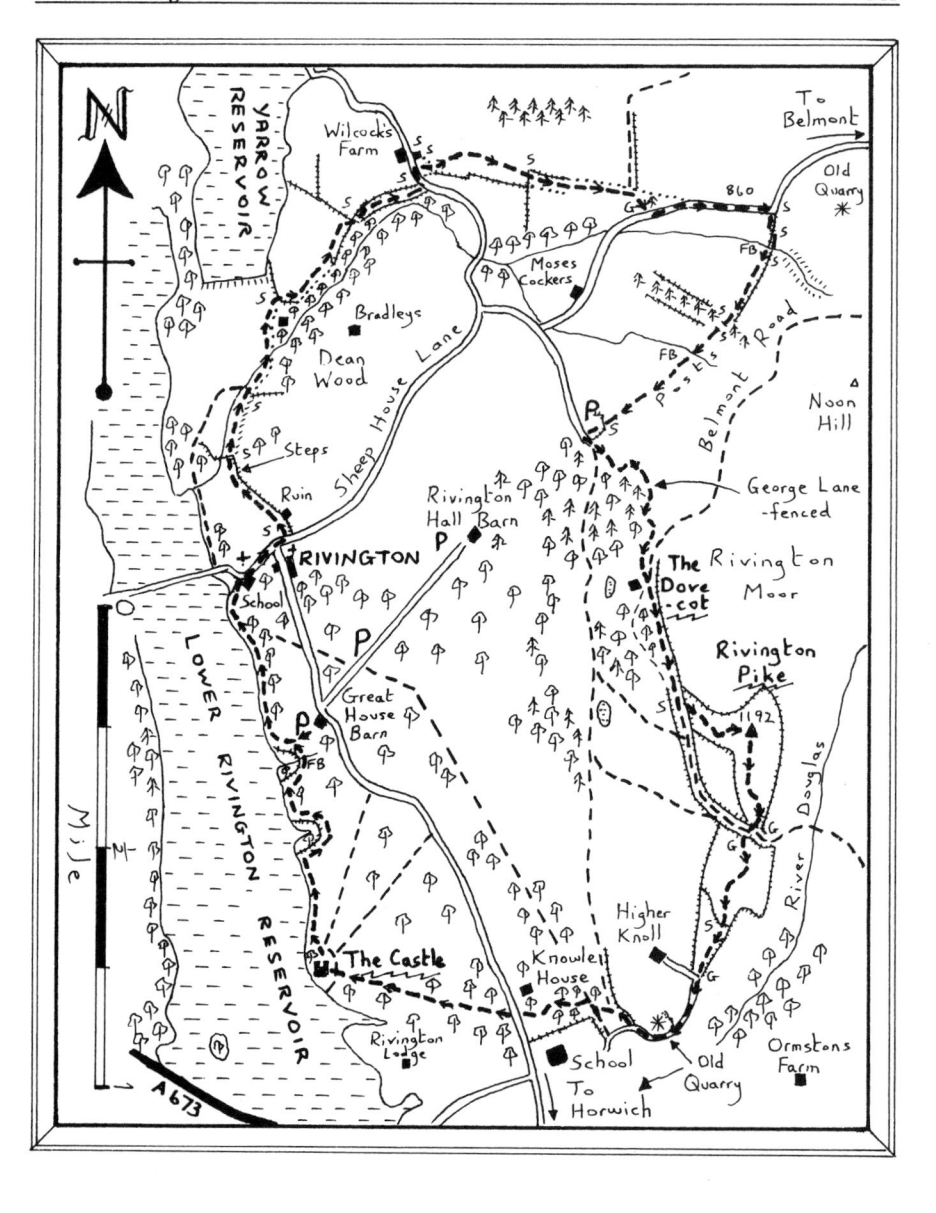

House Lane. A glance across to the right horizon will reveal a tower prodding the sky with its pointed snout. Often mistaken for Rivington Pike, this is, in fact, the celebrated Dovecot.

Walk up the road for 400 metres until it swings sharply to the left. Stride over a stile on the right and descend a steep grass bank to cross a cutting. Halfway down, cross a stile to continue on the far side of the fence then cross the brook by a footbridge. Another stile and footbridge will return you to the right side of the fence so you can continue around the flank of Noon Hill. Negotiate a narrow band of fenced conifers stiled at either side and carry on over another footbridge, dropping gradually down to reach a car park at the end of a metalled lane. Take a left up George's Lane, a rough track winding uphill, to merge with the old road connecting Belmont and Horwich adjacent to the Dovecot.

This odd structure enjoys a similarity with Scottish country houses, which stems from the owner's Highland interests. Tall and narrow with a steeply canted roof, it presents a image of childlike simplicity that is out of character in this remotely austere location perched on the edge of the terraced gardens – truly, a bizarre eccentricity if ever there was one.

Lord Leverhulme's wife used the top floor as a sewing room and enjoyed the distant panorama across West Lancashire. The lower floors were taken over by the stock of pigeons kept by His Lordship. One can only surmise as to whether in the early years of the 20th century, he used them to communicate with his business interests at Port Sunlight. Following many years of neglect, the tower has been renovated in accordance with the modern concern for rustic preservation. Continue along the old road until a stile on the left marks the start of a purpose-built causeway to the summit of Rivington Pike.

Few sites in Lancashire are more prominent and eye-catching, which is no doubt the reason why John Andrews chose the site. Once a beacon lit to warn of traumatic events such as the sighting of the Spanish Armada in 1588, Lord Leverhulme later used it as a shooting lodge. He would often shelter here from the rampant westerlies that beat across the exposed moorland wilderness. Now closed, countless visitors still find their way to the squat tower which even boasts its own fell race and a fair on Good Fridays. The view to the east is dominated by the wild expanse of Winter Hill and the TV mast, the top of which is often obscured by swirling skeins of damp cloud.

Descend the more natural path on the southern slope to a gate that deposits you once again on the old road. Cross to a gate at the far side and continue down a clear track that merges with the paved access road serving Higher Knoll. Follow this road down past an abandoned quarry to a stile at the bottom. Keep ahead on a grass track before dropping down through the trees to join a wide, earthen concourse cutting arrow-straight through the dense woodland of the lower park. Bear right for 100 metres until an obvious track on the left can be followed. This parallels the fenced campus of Rivington and Blackrod High School. Follow it across an open glade and into trees again before emerging onto Rivington Lane, near the entrance to Knowe House.

Cross over and walk along the broad avenue that leads unerringly to Liverpool Castle. This is Lord Leverhulme's second major folly and was intended as an exact replica of the original castle after its despoilation following the Civil War. The ruin was never actually finished but who would ever guess? A plaque at the entrance indicates how the real castle in Liverpool would have looked in all its glory.

In 1967 men working nearby noticed a nebulous figure, starkly white against the dull grey of the walls, flitting amongst the bare ruins. For two hours the mysterious entity glided about as if aimlessly searching before finally disappearing. Could it possibly have been a throwback to a bygone era? A confused spirit trapped within the original essence of Liverpool Castle forever seeking its lost abode. The castle was finally raised to the ground in 1720 as a more contemporary Liverpool developed. With this in mind, head north past the round tower along a thin path that soon joins a clear trail following the edge of the reservoir.

Circle round a fenced wildlife preservation enclave before returning to the water's edge. At the next enclosure, cross a footbridge then leave the lakeside path to strike inland back to Great House Barn car park.

Walk 28. Belmont

Wintering on the Hill

Mysteries: George Henderson GR 661145, Belmont Highwayman

Distance: 4 miles

Total Height Climbed: 750 feet (229 metres)

Nearest Shops: Belmont

Start and Finish: Park on Naylor's Terrace on the west side of Belmont's main street, adjacent to the Black Bull Hotel.

Map: Ordnance Survey 1:25 000 Explorer 19, West Pennine Moors

Although not one of the chocolate box villages that characterise much of the Ribble Valley, Belmont nonetheless has charm and a sense of purpose. Originally known as Hordern meaning 'dirty vale', the present appendage was suggested in 1800 and is infinitely more appropriate. It means 'beautiful mountain'.

Reliant on the textile industry in the early years of its existence, Belmont's mills took advantage of swift-flowing soft water that collected in the Roddlesworth Valley for the development of bleaching and dyeing. Coal-fired engines quickly replaced power from huge waterwheels once the age of steam arrived. It is greatly to the credit of the village that the Belmont Bleaching and Dyeing Company is still in operation, now making use of electrically operated machinery. The brick chimney advertising the company's association with Belmont stands as a testament to the philanthropic endeavour exercised by Edward Deakin. Such halcyon times may be a thing of the past but a sense of traditional pride still emanates from the dark stone terraces that perch on the steep valley slopes.

The Walk

Naylor's Terrace is one such cluster from where our walk commences. At the end of the paved cul-de-sac, continue ahead along a grassy fenced track and out onto the eastern shoulder of Sharples Higher End.

Old Belmont's memorial to a clean, regular water supply

Beyond a stile, keep ahead with a fence on your right to a stepped wall stile. Bear left away from the wall along a clear path slanting over the fell side. A cross wall is soon reached with a wide gap. Surge ahead to pass beneath exposed flakes of sandstone garnished with purple splashes of heather and known as Hoar Stones Brow. Of little account if they were transposed to a more rugged locale, here they assume the proportions of a major rock face. When all around is tough moorland grass, the partial exposure of a naked torso is certain to raise eyebrows.

This path soon merges with the road connecting Rivington and Belmont at a fence stile. Continue up the road for a further 200 metres until a stile is reached on the left at Hordern Stoops. Public access to the Winter Hill moors is provided from here alongside a fence and broken wall. Follow it south in a straight line across swampy tussocks, aiming for the steeply canting platform ahead.

Like alien spacecraft from a distant galaxy, the communication masts, although an intrusion into the natural landscape, are nonetheless unlikely to excite adverse comment. After all, everybody watches TV, don't they?

This yomp over ankle-jarring terrain soon slows to a gentle plod up the final bank alongside the fence. At the ridge crest, negotiate a stile for the stroll along to the highest point. Barely discernible as such on this broad windswept plateau, the trig column is dwarfed by the steel monsters ranged along the paved access road. What ought to be an obvious focal point for itinerant fell-wanderers is lost amid the radio gantries.

Join the road and accompany it round to an iron pillar on the left side. No chance of this rusting monument competing with the hi-tech mast soaring aloft close by, but the plaque erected thereon tells its own poignant story. It was here that a Scots trader journeying from Horwich to Belmont was brutally slain back in 1838. George Henderson was only 20 years of age when robbed and fatally shot on this bleak wilderness. Having failed to reach the Black Dog Inn by the appointed hour, his friend set off through the thick November mist to search for him but was unfortunately too late.

This man was later able to identify a suspicious miner whom he passed carrying a gun, although the fellow was later acquitted due to lack of evidence. So the mysterious assailant of George Henderson was never apprehended and the Scotsman's demise remains unsolved to this day. For some years after a lone piper came onto the moor at the anniversary of George Henderson's death and could be heard playing a sad lament to the memory of his deceased clansman.

But it is the monumental skyscraper that dominates the landscape. Restrained by numerous cables, it appears ready to blast off into orbit at any moment. How could we possibly watch Coronation Street if that were to happen?

Return to the sharp left-hander and fork right over a stile and down a clearly marked path shelving gently down the tussocky flank of Folds Pasture. Unusually at this height, there are small herds of cattle where sheep are normally dominant. After passing through a gap in the wall that scythes across Grange Brow, follow a ledge down the increasingly acute gradient.

On reaching an obvious bifurcation on the left that connects with an old access track to Hill Top, descend it to cross straight over where a fence stile is climbed. Head down the lower pasture, keeping left of String Reservoir. Somewhat indistinct, the path brushes the edge of the tree line to reach the main A675 road.

This was the hunting ground for notorious highwaymen in the 18th century. These villains preyed on unsuspecting travellers who ventured out of Bolton along this lonely stretch of highway. One such felon, Horrocks, had stopped a coach and appropriated a haul of jewellery from the occupants. When disturbed in his criminal endeavour the

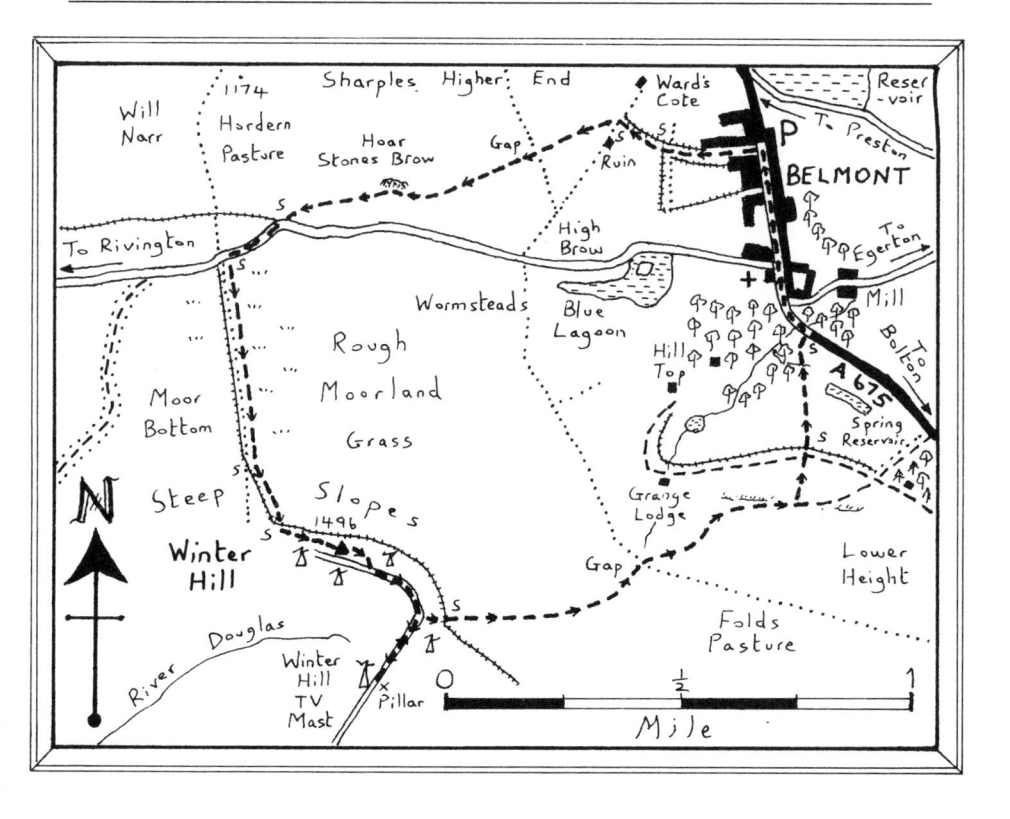

crafty rogue threw his booty into a nearby hollow, intending to retrieve it at some future date when the coast was clear. Unbeknown to him, a certain young man called Grimshaw chanced upon the cache and kept it secret, hoping to make a quick profit for himself. When Grimshaw attempted to sell the jewellery, the police were informed and he was arrested.

Charged with the original crime of highway robbery, his protestations of innocence fell on deaf ears and the ultimate penalty for such a crime was pronounced. Poor Grimshaw was stunned into silence as the judge made the fateful decree that he should be 'hanged by the neck until you are dead and may the Lord have mercy on your soul'. And so in November of 1780, the poor fellow met his untimely end at Preston jail.

A ghostly apparition with a noose around its neck has frequently been observed along this section of road, appearing to emit frightful pleas that he was wrongly condemned. Such entreaties go unheard as the silent spectre searches in vain for the real culprit.

Entering the village of Belmont, the oldest part of Maria Square is soon reached on the right after crossing Egerton Road. This was the centre of village life during the 18th century, when the industrial phase was in its infancy. On the corner stands a stone memorial commemorating a redoubtable victory over the powerful water authority. In 1907 Belmont was provided with a regular supply of clean, piped water from the local reservoirs to replace the inconsistent and often polluted springs and wells used by past generations. Clearly this was an historic and influential outcome for such a small community and a just cause for celebration in this manner.

Continue up the steep main street, passing the Black Dog on your left. Another 300 metres will return you to the Black Bull Hotel, and a welcome tipple if you are so inclined.

Walk 29. Darwen Moor

Moorland Myths

Mysteries: Jubilee Tower GR 679216, The Lyon's Den GR 674204, Hollinshead Well GR 664199

Distance: 5 miles

Total Height Climbed: 600 feet (183 metres)

Nearest Shops: Darwen

Start and Finish: Extensive free parking is available at the Ryal Fold Information Centre, located 1½ miles along the Tockholes road. Turn off the A675 at the only road junction between Belmont and Abbey village.

Map: Ordnance Survey 1:25 000 Explorer 19, West Pennine Moors

As a young sprout of tender years, I often went to Morecambe with my parents on a Sunday outing. Our car journey always took us via Belmont and the West Pennine Moors, and every time I was fascinated by the huge monument perched on the edge of Darwen Moor to the east. Boasting the distinctively finned caste of a sleek spaceship, it evoked colourful images of 'The Eagle''s Dan Dare blasting off in search of the dreaded Mekon. And each time we passed, it was still there. Spare parts problem maybe? Some things never change. In fact, the tower has been on Darwen Moor since 1897 in celebration of Queen Victoria's diamond jubilee so is unlikely to have hit the 'cosmic trail' before you arrive.

The rippling upland country that encompasses the West Pennine Moors separates mill towns and villages where textile manufacture once predominated. Surging streams that fed off the moors turned water wheels before the industry adopted coal as its source of power. Today the smoking chimneys are no more and the towns are much cleaner places in which to live and work. India Mill in Darwen, famous for its chimney designed like the Campanile bell tower in Venice, is a preserved relic of the great age of King Cotton. Most of the other mills have either closed or been turned over to alternative uses. Not so the moorland above. It still remains a bleak, windswept wilderness that offers walkers terrain of the highest quality.

The Walk

Our walk starts from the Information Centre at Ryal Fold, passing the end of Livingstone Terrace through a gate to ascend a clear track. Climbing gradually, we soon arrive at a gate marking the edge of a woodland belt.

Trees slant down into the deep cutting of Stepback Brook and the path slices through the middle to emerge and continue alongside the foaming torrent. Our way bears left over the bridged watercourse, at the far side of which is a stile. Mount a steep path to gain a wider track that climbs to the moorland plateau above. On reaching the first stone marker with Darwen Tower carved on the side, follow the arrow left to a fence stile and then along the edge of the escarpment. When the accompanying fence slants down towards Sunnyhurst Reservoir, our route leans right along the upper rim towards the tower, which overshadows a lowly trig column.

Unlike many similar structures, this one is a true 'prospect tower' and open all year round for the public to enter. Climb the stone stairway that circles to the lower viewing platform before mounting an increasingly constricted flue that culminates in a narrow iron spiral. A door gives onto the upper stage, which is surmounted by a copper dome and weather vane. On a clear day one's endeavour is rewarded with distant views of Snowdon and the Isle of Man, not forgetting Blackpool Tower. No such luck on my visit when a grey pall hung low over the horizon.

It is perhaps significant that this supernovic edifice also celebrated the opening up of the moor to general access. Only during the previous year of 1896 had vigorous public protest resulted in legislation guaranteeing free movement along the public footpaths that criss-cross the area. Thousands swarmed up on to the newly opened moor to celebrate the dual event.

By the 1960s, unfortunately, the tower had become a rather sad affair and was in danger of collapsing due to neglect. Only after it had been designated as of architectural and historical importance, in keeping with India Mill and its chimney clearly visible in the valley below, was the money raised to have it refurbished. Both buildings now make fine ambassadors for the town of Darwen. Having attempted to identify other more distant landmarks, carefully descend the steeply spiralling steps and head due south along a clear path.

Plans to develop fifteen windmills here on Darwen Moor are more controversial and likely to cause heated debate for some time (September 1998). Hopefully the matter will have been amicably settled when

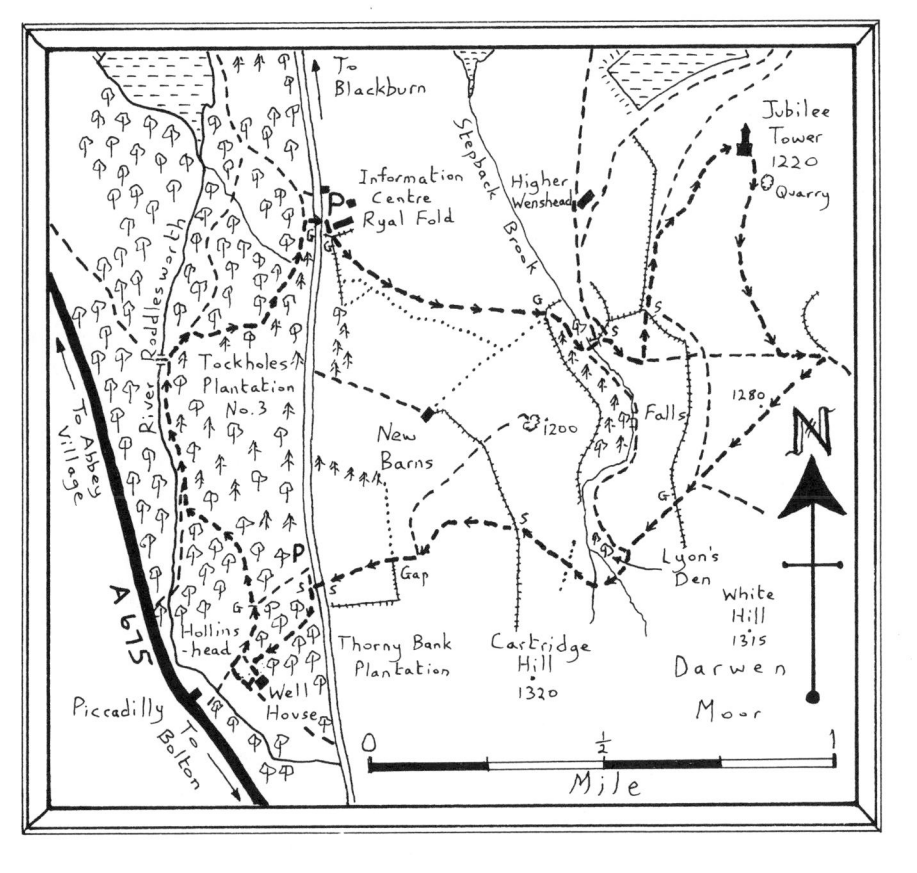

you pass a deep hole on the left where stone for the erection of the tower was quarried.

Press on over a slight rise and so arrive at a T-junction. Make a left for 100 metres until a broken fence is reached on the eastern flank overlooking Darwen. Head sharp right along a grassy track that makes a direct crossing of the domed wilderness. Eventually arriving at a fence, pass through the gate and continue ahead, slanting right to a small isolated group of trees adjacent to Stepback Brook.

Grassed over foundations of an old cottage are all that remains of what has become known as The Lyon's Den. Here it was that in the late 18th century John Lyon built a turf house from which to tend his sheep. A huge giant over 7ft tall, he would manfully struggle to enter his primitive hovel. Once when three men were passing on their way to Darwen, then merely a village, they saw him crawling out and exclaimed,

'See...he's coming out of the Lyon's Den!' And so the lonely spot was christened. Certainly a pleasant nook to recline over lunch before rejoining the path to circle right to a fence on the near horizon.

Climb a stile to descend the north shoulder of Cartridge Hill on a path that loops down to cross a narrow rill through a gap. Keep going ahead to gain the road over a stile. Cross straight over, mounting a wall stile on the far side to enter Thorny Bank Plantation. Bear left alongside the wall until the path angles right into the depths of the forest. Make a gradual descent, soon emerging from the trees close to the ruins of Hollinshead Hall. Today only the stone edgings of the outbuildings remain. The hall itself was built on a raised dais to the left, of which there are no visible remnants.

Step back into the pages of history to a period when the Hollinshead family owned considerable tracts of land hereabouts. When the last in line died in 1858 the house fell into disrepair, the stone eventually being commandeered by local farmers. One unusual feature that has been preserved lies tucked away in a corner close to the site of the old house. Nobody has been able to positively assert how the Well House was used. Many claim it was a buttery for keeping dairy products cool, others that it served a more abstruse purpose, the waters possessing magical properties that could cure all manner of ills. Known as 'The Holy Spring' in the 19th century, it was visited by pilgrims keen to attain spiritual union. Or perhaps it was merely a reliable water supply as five springs are known to feed into the well. Whatever its origins, this fascinating place is well worthy of investigation.

From the environs of Hollinshead Hall, head right along a clear track (initially walled) to a gate. The track heading right leads back to Slipper Lowe car park. Our route continues ahead, slanting down into the heavily wooded valley of the River Roddlesworth. The path makes a gradual descent to a footbridge where numerous paths branch off. Here we veer right uphill and away from the river until a junction is reached after 100 metres. Take the narrower path forking right to climb up through Tockholes No.3 Plantation, emerging from the tree cover by a gate. Go right to join the road opposite the visitor centre.

This is an easygoing walk on clear paths. There is much to see and even more to think about on this splendid outing into the heart of the Lancashire moorlands.

Darwen Tower – a memorial to Queen Victoria's Diamond Jubilee

Walk 30. Holcombe Moors

Strange Murder

Mysteries: Ellen Smith GR 776192; Pilgrim Stone GR 771182; Peel Monument GR 778164

Distance: 5½ miles

Total Height Climbed: 450 feet (137 metres)

Nearest Shops: Ramsbottom

Start and Finish: A free car park is provided on the east side of the B6214 at Holcombe.

Map: Ordnance Survey 1:25 000 Explorer 19, West Pennine Moors

Rising out of the Irwell Valley on its western flank, a tract of bleak grass moorland offers walking territory of supreme quality. Holcombe Moor has long been a favourite spot for locals to escape the drudgery created by smoky mill towns such as Ramsbottom and Bury. But not only the cotton spinners enjoyed the chance to stride out across the open wilderness, even a Prime Minister claimed it for a memorial to his achievements. Dominating the view for miles around, there can be no disputing the esteem in which Victorian society held its leaders. And the Peel Monument makes a lasting testament to the man who will forever be remembered for creating the world-renowned British 'bobby'.

The disturbing element associated with Holcombe is its use by the military. Army manoeuvres are a regular feature of the area and announced by the raising of red flags and discharge of loud noises. Thankfully it is the western side of the moor that is most affected.

The Walk

From the car park, cross the B6214 and take a narrow passage between wall and fence that links with the old cobbled highway after 100 metres. Bear right along this route until it merges with the modern alternative. Our route forks left behind an old stone building to climb above Holcombe village. Once open country is reached, the track opens out with an accompanying wall on the right only. Passing Higher Tops, this lonely trail is typical of those travelled by the majority in the days when movement between settlements was a serious affair and not to be undertaken lightly. The next farm is Chatterton Close, where a gate is opened. The track continues down a walled passage with another gate at the end.

After this, we pass a tree-lined vale on the right as the path kinks to the right past a gravel pit. Carry on for a further quarter mile until the second of two fences is passed on the right, just beyond Broadwood Edge Farm. Fork left along an indistinct bifurcation to meet the path approaching from Helmshore by a wall.

Head left up the gently rising swell of Beetle Hill, bearing away from the chaperoning presence of the wall to encounter a distinctive upright stone adjoining a cairn of stones. Emblazoned with the carved form of a young girl and the initials 'ES', it marks the gruesome site of a most despicable murder committed in the year 1735.

Ellen Strange and her sweetheart, a pedlar by the name of Billy, set off from Hawkshaw to visit the fair at Haslingden. The most direct route was across Holcombe Moor on this very same footpath. On their return the pair stopped at the White Horse in Helmshore. Copious draughts of

Site of a heinous murder on lonely Holcombe Moor

the local ale no doubt inflamed the young man's passion. He clearly expected to have his way with the winsome Ellen as they recrossed the desolate stretch of moorland. Could it be that his amorous intentions were repulsed, at which point the pedlar's restraint snapped with fatal consequences? That seems to be the most likely scenario. The craven blackguard was soon arrested and quickly confessed, hoping for leniency. But it was not to be and the law took its full and terminal course.

He was hanged at Lancaster Castle and his body taken back to Bull Hill, there to be strung up in chains on a gibbet for the birds to peck. As a dire warning to others that could not control their lusty appetites, it was a success as no further incidents of the sort were reported thereafter. A military presence has been present on Holcombe Moor since the Civil War in the 1640s and perhaps the dangling corpse of young Billy the pedlar was used for target practice.

Ponder on these events as you carry on along the path, rising gently past a broken walled enclosure on the left. Soon a notice announcing the possibility of military action is passed. So, if the flag is flying: **duck!** Otherwise continue ahead as the path crosses a shallow depression and the monument known as The Pilgrim's Cross is reached.

The cross disappeared over a century ago to be replaced by the present squat edifice complete with carved inscription to the memory of pilgrims who passed this way. After resting and offering up prayers on this site, the monks continued their journey to Whalley Abbey in the Ribble Valley. The foundation is reputedly the original stone from the 12th century, which the Vicar of Holcombe resurrected in 1901.

The main path over this desolate saddle continues onward down into the valley of Red Brook. Our route forks left along the crest of the broad ridge over a subsidiary rise before crossing the highest point on Harcles Hill. Drop down a steep bank and cross a narrow stream in the depression before carrying on to reach the fence surrounding Peel Monument.

A double gate, weighted to ensure its closure, is clearly designed to restrain creatures of the moor. But all eyes will inevitably be drawn to the towering monolith of dark, weathered gritstone which stands 128ft (39 metres) in height. Teetering on the edge of an abrupt downfall that encloses the southern extremity of Holcombe Moor, it has been refurbished and is now apparently open to the public. But only on certain days as I discovered recently.

Opened in 1852 at a cost of £1000, the stone used was quarried from the huge hole alongside. Victorian dignitaries lived according to the

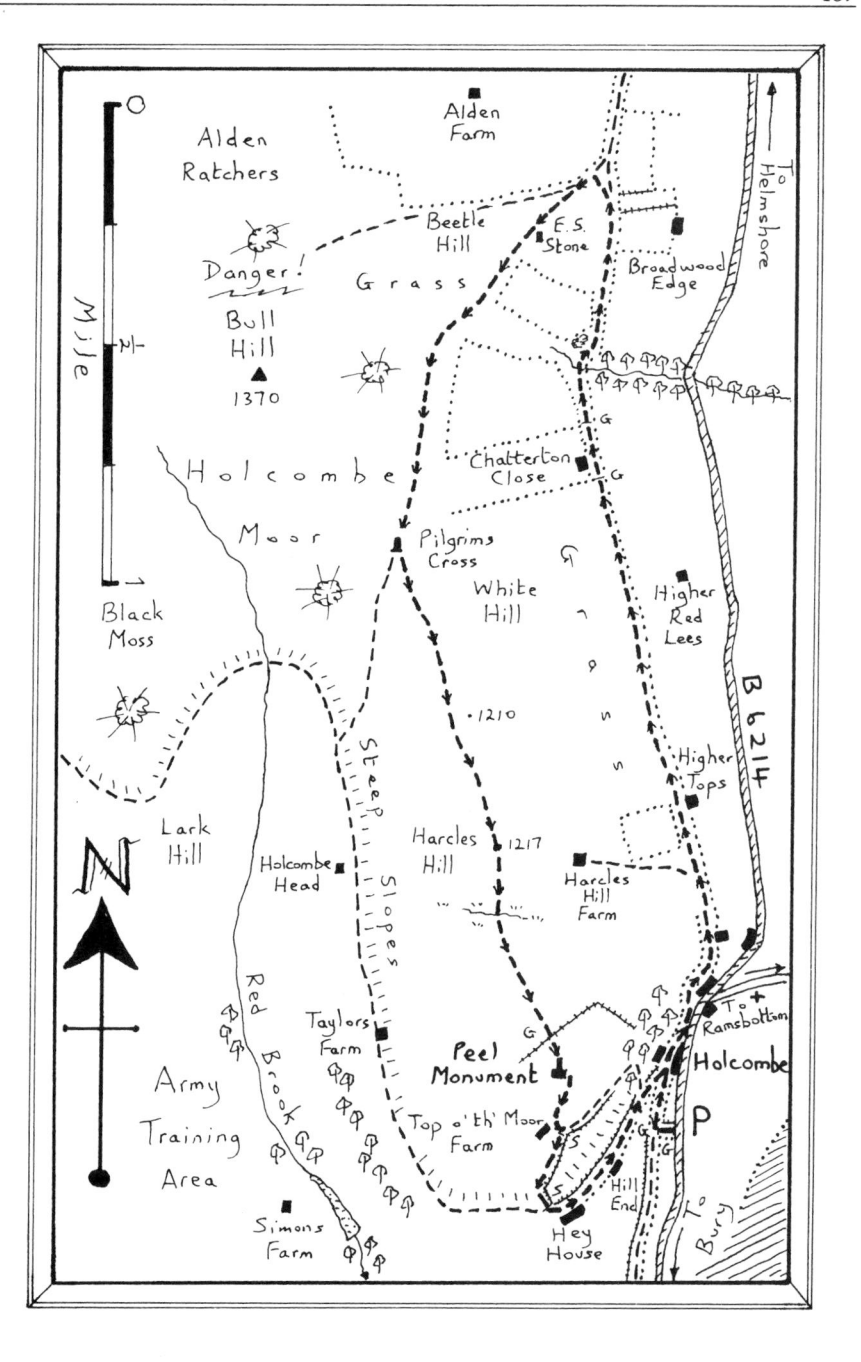

grand style of the times and in stark contrast to the factory workers. A natural progression was to erect these mighty structures in their memory.

From the tower, head south down a sloping track of gravel towards Top o' th' Moor Farm. When it swings sharply to the left, continue ahead over a stile and accompany a fence along the steep lip of the escarpment. The fence soon slants down to a farm track skirting the lower slopes of the fell. Bear left past Hey House and Hill End to arrive at a junction and the cobbled road encountered at the start. Take a right to retrace your steps back to the short, gated passage that will return you to the car park.

Enjoy this easy walk in an anti-clockwise direction over desolate moorland that is within a stone's throw of dense urban development. The rights of passage have been in use for centuries and can probably tell many stories that time has erased from the landscape. So when the keen wind howls through the tough sedges and a dank mist smothers the moor in its foetid embrace, give thanks for the clear trails that have been stamped out.

Also of interest . . .

WALKS IN MYSTERIOUS SOUTH LAKELAND

Old Nick, witches, wizards monsters, fairies, and grizzly monsters! Graham Dugdale intertwines intriguing tales of these dark beings with his 30 skilfully chosen gentle walks in south Cumbria. "This is a well-researched guide book, well written, with a welcome thread of humour." THE GREAT OUTDOORS. £6.95

WALKS IN MYSTERIOUS NORTH LAKELAND

Also by Graham Dugdale, an unusual collection of 30 walks which provide a unique opportunity to visit places with a strange and mythical history. "Each Walk.. features remarkable hand-drawn maps and stylish, entertaining writing that is almost as good to read before a roaring open fire as on the open fells" LAKELAND WALKER. 'Graham writes with robust enthusiasm...colourful excursions' KESWICK REMINDER £6.95

WALKS IN MYSTERIOUS WILTSHIRE

Step into secret Wiltshire, one of the most mysterious of English counties, containing Stonehenge, Avebury, several white horses and now seasonally visited by crop circles! Laurence Main's 27 routes, suitable for all ages and abilities, take you into enchanting walking countryside, and a world of discovery. £6.95

WALKS IN MYSTERIOUS OXFORDSHIRE

Follow the leylines that connect holy hills and sacred sites, search for a lost giant, explore the river dedicated the goddess Isis and follow the spirit path to Banbury Cross, where the white horse overlooks Uffington. "...an attractively presented book which makes you want to pull your boots on and start exploring" BOOTPRINT. £6.95